Immigration Guide to the
USA

D1057349

Published by How To Books Ltd,
3 Newtec Place, Magdalen Road,
Oxford OX4 1RE. United Kingdom.
Tel: (01865) 793806. Fax: (01865) 248780.
email: info@howtobooks.co.uk
www.howtobooks.co.uk

First published 1999
Second edition 2002
Third edition 2004
Fourth edition 2006

All rights reserved. No part of this work may be
reproduced or stored in an information retrieval
system (other than for purposes of review) without
the express permission of the publisher in writing.

© Copyright 2006 Henry G. Liebman

British Library Cataloguing in Publication Data
A catalogue record for this book is available from the
British Library

Produced for How To Books by Deer Park Productions
Typeset by Anneset Productions, Weston-super-Mare, Somerset
Cover design by Baseline Arts Ltd., Oxford
Printed and bound by Cromwell Press, Trowbridge, Wiltshire

NOTE: The material contained in this book is set out
in good faith for general guidance and no liability
can be accepted for loss or expense incurred as a
result of relying in particular circumstances on
statements made in the book. The laws and regulations are complex and liable to change, and readers
should check the current position with the relevant
authorities before making personal arrangements.

Contents

About the author   xi
Preface   xv

1 The history of US immigration   **1**
    The first attempts at limiting immigrants   1
    Understanding the modern immigration system   2
    Taking new steps to curtail 'illegals'   3

2 Understanding the background and basics of visas   **6**
    What is a visa?   6
    Two categories of visas   6
    Understanding how the USCIS and Consuls
        evaluate visa petitions   8
    Getting the green light to enter   9
    Form I-94 and visa expiration dates   9
    Being denied entry: your options   10
    Change of status and extension of stay   11
    Visa revalidation   12
    North American Free Trade Acts visas   12
    Summary   13
    Basic concepts of non immigrant visas   13

3 Using a B-1 visa   **16**
    Applying for entry on a B-1 visa   16
    What constitutes work?   17
    Application procedures and strategy   18

4 Travelling for pleasure: The B-2 visa   **20**
    Identifying problem areas   20

Students   20
Young adults   21

5 **Entering the US as a fiancé(e)**   **23**
The fiancé(e) visa category   24
Following procedures   24
Summary   25

6 **Temporary working visas**   **26**
Getting the general outline   26
Understanding the terminology   27
L visas: Intra-company Transfer   28
Treaty trader/investor basic terminology   29
Control and ownership of a US treaty company   32
Treaty trader: E-1 visa   32
Treaty investor E-2   34
Basic requirements of H-1B visas:
    For professional workers   34
Professional licences   37
Knowing when to use H, L or E   40
Summarising eligibility for E, H and L visa holders   41

7 **Sending staff to a new business in America**   **42**
Establishing the US company first   42
Forming the corporation   43
Finding premises for doing business   44
Applying for the working visa   44
Case study   44
Exploring alternatives to the L-1A approach   46
Making the final choice   47
Extending your US stay after the one year period   48
Passing the one year of business hurdle   49
What about the children?   50
Exploring the alternatives   51

8 **Staffing an existing US business**   **52**
Choosing the correct visa   52
Managers   53
H-1B visas   55
Common applications of H-1 visas   57
Engineers   58

Specialised knowledge and essential skills   60
Recruitment difficulties   63
Other H-2B applications   63
Review of guidelines for specialists   65
Balancing foreign and US employment   65
Preventing the discrimination lawsuit   66

9 Five ways to obtain a green card   68
Understanding general concepts   69
Being interviewed for permanent residence status   72
Choosing between adjustment of status and
    consular processing   73
Working during the adjustment of status
    processing   74
Green card categories   74
Planning for the quota waiting period   75
Investing in America for a green card   79
Paying by cash or credit   80
The regional centre programme   82
Summarising the immigrant investment category   85
Retiring in America: The 'two-step' method for
    managers, executives and entrepreneurs   85
Details of the two-step process   87
Another two-step approach   90
Timing and procedure   92
Attending the green card interview   93
Looking at the green card   93
Travelling during the USCIS interview process   94
Avoiding common pitfalls   95
Conclusion   95
Those with extraordinary abilities in sciences,
    arts and business   96
Qualifying for national interest exemption   96
The last resort: Labour Certification   98
Keeping your green card   105
Cheap tax planning   108
Permits to re-enter   108
Applying for a social security number   110
Summary   111

10 Obtaining student visas   **112**
Attending public schools   112
Filing for your student visa   113
Travelling on a student visa   113
Proving financial support   114
Strict enforcement   114
Three key questions, the same answer: Yes   115
Working while studying   115
Post-completion practical training programme   116
Options after practical training   117

**11 Visas for the privileged, media, athletes,
      entertainers, cultural exchanges, religious
      workers and tycoons**   **118**
I visa for information media   118
O visa, a mini green card for outstanding actors,
      business people and artists   119
Working as an athlete or entertainer   120
Q visa for cultural exchange programmes   120
R visa for religious workers   121
Details about NAFTA   123

12 Naturalisation: Becoming an American citizen   **126**
Literacy requirement   126
Civics requirement   127
Advantages of citizenship   127
Dual citizenship   127
The qualifying period   128
The citizenship test   128
Obtaining a certificate of naturalisation   129
Practical pointers for naturalisation applicants   130

**13 Thoughts for human resource managers and
      employees**   **131**
Why send an employee overseas?   131
Understanding why employees want to go abroad   132
Easing the transition to overseas life   132
Relocation tips for company employees and
      individuals   134

Appendix 1 – Immigration forms and other
  documents   136
Appendix 2 – Visa categories   139
Appendix 3 – Important addresses   142
Appendix 4 – Suggested document lists   144
Appendix 5 – Typical citizenship questions   148

Glossary   155

Index   158

About the Author

Henry Liebman is a 54-year-old attorney living and practising law in Seattle, Washington. After serving as a tax specialist for Touche Ross and Company, he became an associate for Franklin and Watkins Attorneys at Law and a member of the Board of Directors of Northwest International Bank. He then joined Franco, Asia, Bensussen. Henry Liebman is now managing partner in Liebman-Mimbu, PLLC, Attorneys at Law. He is founder and director of Northwest International Bank; Founder and President of American Life Inc., a company servicing the needs of immigrant investors and Director of the Economic Development Council of Seattle and King County. He travels extensively to Asia and Europe in conjunction with his legal practice. He has two children, Rachel and Catherine, and his recreational pursuits include golf, hiking, mountain-climbing and world-wide travel.

LEGAL ASSISTANCE

There are many law firms able to help with your immigration needs. The author's Seattle-based firm, Liebman-Mimbu, PLLC, was first established in 1904, and provides legal services to an international clientele. One of the founders, Albert M. Franco, who has practised law since 1940, led the US Army G-2 in Kobe, Japan, immediately following World War II, and served as a consultant to the US Agency for International Development in Central and Latin Americas. Two members of the firm have served as Legislative Assistants to the US House of Representatives. Firm partner and author, Henry G. Liebman, concentrates on international legal matters and manages the firm's international and immigration law practice. He is the Business Immigration Ombudsman for PACE, a tri-lateral trade council for owners and managers of small- and mid-sized companies in Canada, the US and Mexico.

Main office
Liebman-Mimbu, PLLC, Attorneys at Law
3223 3rd Avenue South, Suite 200
Seattle, WA 98134
Tel: (206) 381 3375
Fax: (206) 381 3376
email: henry@usa-immigration.com
www: usa-immigration.com-homepage

Special thanks to Karyne Pesho and Robert Mimbu, my colleagues, who reviewed the drafts for this book and made sure the updates were complete and correct.

Due to the many changes in the names of various departments involved with the immigration process including the US Citizenship and Immigration Services (legacy INS) and Customs and Border Patrol, all of which fall under the Department of Homeland Security, we have used USCIS as a generic term, covering all relevant entities.

Preface

The United States and Canada accept more immigrants today than since the early 1900s. Several million tourists, temporary workers, asylum seekers, refugees and permanent residents come to North America each year. America's 'melting pot' and Canada's 'mosaic', once almost entirely European, now include people from every corner of the planet. People move to North America for freedom, safety and opportunity, while appreciating the unique blend of living space, political stability and high standard of living.

North America is relatively open to immigrants. However, as the continent fills with new arrivals, the doors will slowly close. During the first 150 years of its history the US accepted whoever arrived. Since the 1920s, American immigration laws have regulated and prioritised the flow of immigrants. Immigrating to the US now requires foreigners seeking entry to position themselves in the most advantageous immigrant categories.

SIMPLIFYING A COMPLEX SUBJECT

After practising immigration law for 22 years, I have found that most clients pose the same questions. Businessmen needing to bring critical personnel to the US typically ask: 'How do I get my workers into the US? How long does it take? And how much will it cost?' Almost everyone wants to know, 'How do I get a green card?'

Mere regurgitation of US immigration laws confuses

clients. Most people want to know the steps required to immigrate, their options, how long the process takes, and their chances for success. They want the information presented in a simple, logical way. This book simplifies the complex subject in a way which I hope you'll find understandable and accessible. It discusses immigration strategies for most scenarios. There are many confusing paths leading to a green card – the nonimmigrant visa list starts at 'A' and ends at 'S'. The list includes diplomats, vessel crew members, UN officials, NATO generals and staff, religious workers, as well as the more commonly used working visas. This book concisely points out the obstacles often encountered with an immigration scenario, and provides solutions.

- It explains how to obtain the best visa for your purposes – for work, investment, study in universities, or permanent residence.

- It teaches you how to interact with US Citizenship and Immigration Services (USCIS) inspectors at border crossings and airports.

- It provides pointers for effective communication with consular officers when applying for visas abroad.

- It provides citizenship questions and answers for those who wish to complete the immigration process.

After reading this book, you'll be able to choose the best immigration strategy to accomplish your ultimate goal. You may be confident enough to handle your own case, or be able to tell your lawyer what you hope to accomplish.

One thing this book doesn't discuss in great detail is J exchange visitor visas. The US Embassy supplies a list of qualified exchange visitor sponsoring organisations. Those organisations will process your J visa and give you more details concerning the procedure than we can in the space allocated in this book.

Henry G. Liebman

1

The History of US Immigration

For all practical purposes, the US had open borders until 1875. Many states actually promoted immigration as the US needed settlers to tame the North American wilderness, and most of the new arrivals came from Northern Europe.

The first serious attempts to limit immigration occurred through a series of laws enacted between 1875 and 1917. These laws excluded lunatics, convicts, all Chinese peoples, beggars, anarchists, and carriers of contagious diseases. Immigrants during this period were assessed a 50-cents-per-person tax.

At the onset of the 20th century, the US received upwards of one million immigrants per year. Most of the new arrivals came from Eastern and Southern Europe, and tended to be Roman Catholic, Eastern Orthodox or Jewish, instead of belonging to America's predominant religion at that time, Protestant Christianity. Many newcomers couldn't read or speak English.

THE FIRST ATTEMPTS AT LIMITING IMMIGRANTS

A series of laws enacted between 1917 and 1924 attempted to limit the number of new immigrants. These laws expanded the categories of excludable aliens, established the **quota system**, and banned all Asians except Japanese, who had made a 'gentleman's agreement' with the US.

The quota system restricted the number of **visas** made available to particular nationalities. The system, which allocated visas according to the number of persons of the same nationality living in the US, favoured the majority

ethnic groups, namely the Northern Europeans. The quota
system limited the total visas issued to 150,000 per year,
with no restrictions on persons born in the Western
Hemisphere. Additionally, the US Congress decided to bar
citizenship to 'Orientals', which meant that Asians,
including Japanese, could no longer become US citizens.

By 1924, US immigration law limited the total number
of aliens and imposed qualitative restrictions.

UNDERSTANDING THE MODERN IMMIGRATION SYSTEM

The next major change in immigration law occurred with
the 1952 Act, which established the modern immigration
system. The new quota system created limits on a per-
country basis without regard to the number of persons of
particular nationalities currently living in the US. Asian
immigration was limited, rather than restricted.

The 1952 Act also established the **preference system**
that gave priority to family members and people with
special skills. This was the first attempt to target
immigrants with special skills.

Subsequent changes to the immigration laws were
driven by a more enlightened attitude toward civil rights.
Positive changes were also due to the increasing need for
US multinational corporations to attract skilled labour, and
to transfer key personnel between the US and foreign
operations.

In 1968 Congress officially abolished restrictions on
Asian immigration. It also eliminated immigration
discrimination based on race, place of birth, sex and
residence. In 1970 Congress implemented the L-1 – or
managerial-transfer – programme. In 1976 Congress
eliminated preferential treatment for residents of the
Western Hemisphere.

TAKING NEW STEPS TO CURTAIL 'ILLEGALS'

By 1986 the US was facing the biggest immigration wave since the turn of the century. Only this time the majority of immigrants were from Latin America and Asia. The West Coast of the US and the border states with Mexico and Cuba bore the brunt of these new arrivals. By some estimates, the number of 'illegals' exceeded the number of legal immigrants.

In 1986 changes to the immigration laws were intended to tighten up the system. Congress legalised hundreds of thousands of illegal immigrants, while introducing the employer-sanctions programme which fines employers for hiring illegal workers. To curtail an epidemic of bogus marriages to US citizens, Congress passed tough laws to prevent marriage fraud.

Current limitations

While the 1986 Act focused on curtailing illegal immigration, the 1990 Act was aimed at helping US businesses attract skilled foreign workers. The 1990 Act established an annual limit of 675,000 permanent resident visas; 465,000 for family class; 140,000 for employment-based categories; and 55,000 for the visa lottery. On top of these limits, the law permits 125,000 refugees and smaller groups authorised by prior laws.

The 1990 Act also increased the number of employment-based visas from approximately 54,000 annually to 140,000 a year. The expanded business-class categories favour persons who make educational, professional, or financial contributions. For example, the 1990 Act created the Immigrant Investor Program. Conversely, the 1990 Act limited the number of non-immigrant visas available to professional workers to 65,000 per year. So far, most of the quota or numerical limitations of the 1990 Act for non-immigrant visas have not been reached.

The tragedy of September 11 caused a rethinking of the US
Citizenship and Immigration Services (USCIS) admission
policies as well as a reorganisation of the USCIS itself. The
USCIS along with several other law enforcement agencies
merged into a new Homeland Security Department on March
1, 2003. USCIS's functions are shared among themselves, the
Bureau of Immigration and Customs Enforcement and the
Bureau of Customs and Border Patrol (USCIS).

One should be aware of the following changes in USCIS
policies:

B1/2 visas for temporary business and pleasure will, except
in cases where more time is clearly necessary, be restricted to
one month time in the US rather than the pre-9/11 six months.
Extensions of time while in the US will be denied more often
to force people to leave and face inspection at consular posts
or at airports or land borders.

Temporary visitors trying to change to student status will be
highly scrutinised and most likely denied unless they were
admitted as an intending student. Remember, USCIS approved
Mohammed Atta's student visa posthumously, after he flew the
plane into the World Trade Center. Some reform is in order.

Generally speaking, changes of status within the US will be
highly scrutinised and denied more often than before 9/11.
Aliens from suspect countries may have to register with local
USCIS offices and report their whereabouts periodically.

These are the more important changes in policy, but not a
definitive list. USCIS policy has been changing almost daily.
It's best to check the USCIS website, Department of State
website or an immigration professional if you intend to come
to the US and may have to ask for an extension of time or
change of status to a different visa category.

Overall, we can expect continued pressure to reduce the
numbers of immigrants, while at the same time improving the
quality of their skills. Family class categories may be limited
to immediate family members, while higher educational and/or
experience requirements may be imposed on professional
workers. There may be more encouragement for foreign
investors.

The beauty of American immigration law is that the US

has moved from an ethnically biased system which favoured Northern Europeans to one that is truly multinational, and allows freedom and opportunity for all. The US offers the only immigration policy in the world that is blind to race, religion, creed and colour. It's truly a unique social experiment which continues to evolve.

2

Understanding the Background and Basics of Visas

WHAT IS A VISA?

A visa – usually stamped in a passport – permits the bearer to apply for entry into a country. The US requires visas, unless a country qualifies for a **visa waiver**. Most European countries, and Japan, qualify for visa waivers. A visa waiver eliminates the visa requirement for business and pleasure trips under 90 days in duration.

Those who plan to work in the US need a visa regardless of how long they intend to remain in the county.

Foreigners living in the US for indefinite periods need a **green card**, or **permanent residence visa**.

TWO CATEGORIES OF VISAS

Visas are either **nonimmigrant**, *ie* temporary, or **immigrant**, *ie* permanent. Refer to the Glossary for a list of the visa categories and the appropriate chapters for full details.

Nonimmigrant visas

The holder of a nonimmigrant visa agrees to leave the US prior to the end of a permitted stay period. The US issues over 30 types of nonimmigrant visas designated by letters of the alphabet. The nonimmigrant visa holder may only engage in the approved activity or work for the petitioning employer. Validity periods vary with the type of nonimmigrant.

Immigrant visas

An immigrant visa permits the holder to live in the US for as long as the US is the permanent place of residence. Immigrant visa holders may engage in any activity and work for any employer without restrictions. The USCIS issues immigrant visa holders with an **Alien Registration Card** as evidence of permanent residence status. The card, now pearl white, and scheduled to change again, was originally green, hence its name: the green card.

Green card holders enjoy all the rights and obligations of citizens except that they cannot vote, and are ineligible to receive some welfare benefits. Green card holders may apply for citizenship after the passage of three years for spouses of US citizens and five years for all other green card holders. Green card holders must file US income tax returns and, in the case of war, serve in the US armed forces if called to duty.

Who processes visas?

Overseas, foreign service officers and US consular posts issue all visas; you must obtain your first visa from a consular officer outside the US. These consuls work for the **Department of State**, an agency of the federal government that controls foreign affairs. Each US consular post determines its own filing procedures, and not all consular posts process visas. Ask the consular post nearest your home for its procedures before applying.

Most visa categories require USCIS approval of a visa petition, or before application at the consulate for a visa stamp. The USCIS, which is part of the Homeland Security Department, approves visa petitions but cannot issue visas.

Not every visa category requires USCIS pre-approval. Exceptions include:

- B-1/B-2 Temporary Business or Tourist Visas
- E-1/2 Treaty Trader/Investor
- I Information Media
- R Religious Workers

• Select categories pertaining to diplomats, military personnel and special cases.

USCIS pre-approval

In order to obtain USCIS visa approval, file your petition and supporting documents by mail or courier with one of the USCIS Regional Processing Centers in Vermont, Texas, Nebraska or California. (See Appendices for addresses.) The USCIS will render its decision by mail. There is nobody to talk to about your petition. The entire process is done in writing. If the USCIS approves your petition, take the approval notice (Form I-797), Consular Visa Application (Form DS-156) and your passport to the US consulate in your area to apply for the visa.

Consular processing

Consuls decide who receives a visa. The consul may accept a USCIS pre-approval, or the officer may ask you for more information, conduct an interview, or deny your visa application. The consul may deny your visa application even though the USCIS approved the petition. Normally the consul will issue the visa petition according to the USCIS approval. Upon approval the consul places the visa stamp in your passport. The stamp shows the place and date of issue, the number of permitted entries, duration, visa type and if applicable, the name of the US employer.

UNDERSTANDING HOW THE USCIS AND CONSULS EVALUATE VISA PETITIONS

The USCIS adjudicates visa petitions solely upon the information contained in the forms, the cover letter and supporting documents. The USCIS makes no personal contact with the applicant. The consulate bases its decision upon the same criteria, except that it may request a personal interview. As a rule, consulates request interviews only when they suspect a problem. Both USCIS and consular applications require detailed documentation.

GETTING THE GREEN LIGHT TO ENTER

Once you have your visa you may apply for entry to the US. The USCIS controls who enters the US just as the consuls control who receives visas. The USCIS may deny your entry to the US even if you have a valid visa.

If the USCIS admits you into the US it will stamp your **Arrival Departure Card** (Form I-94) with the date of entry, visa type and expiration date. The I-94 card issued by the USCIS determines how long you may stay in the US. Airline flight attendants distribute I-94 cards before landing at an international airport.

FORM I-94 AND VISA EXPIRATION DATES

The **expiration dates** on the I-94 card and your visa may differ. The I-94 expiration date determines how long you may stay in the US, while the visa merely indicates the time period during which you may apply for entry. For example, a **multiple entry visa**, valid for three years, permits unlimited applications to enter the US during the three-year visa validity period.

You must leave the US or extend your I-94 by its expiration date even if your visa is valid beyond that period. For example, you have a three-year visa but the USCIS only admits you for two years. In other words, the I-94 form expires before the visa does. In this case you must leave the US, or extend your I-94 form, prior to the I-94 expiration date even though you have a valid visa.

Overstaying expiration dates

Failure to leave the US on or before the I-94 expiration date results in the automatic cancellation of your visa. Because the US does not have a reliable system for matching entrance and exit dates, USCIS inspectors allow 48 hours from the I-94 expiration date to enter another country. If your passport does not contain a timely entry stamp, or another proof of entry to another country, you may be denied later re-entry to the US. Because many countries do not routinely stamp passports, those who wish to return to the US on the same visa should make sure their passports are stamped or retain the airline tickets.

Overstays must apply for a new visa in their home country. To further complicate matters, consuls generally deny visas to persons who overstayed without a compelling reason. Compelling reasons include cancelled airline flights, sickness, death and emergencies.

People who overstay for six months up to one year may not re-enter the US for three years. Those who overstay for one year or more may not re-enter the US for ten years. Exceptions are made in cases of family emergency or extreme hardship to separated family members.

BEING DENIED ENTRY: YOUR OPTIONS

Summary removal procedures give the USCIS the right to deny entry to anybody they feel is misrepresenting the purpose of their stay in the US, such as persons holding tourist visas intending to work or to marry in the US. There is no right to a hearing or appeal and the applicant for entry may be barred from coming to the US for five years.

The USCIS may, in its sole discretion, merely exclude an applicant from entering the US without summary removal. This means the applicant for entry is sent home on the next flight but is not barred from further entry to the US. Alternatively, the USCIS may allow the applicant the right to a hearing.

The summary removal proceedings were designed to deter people who enter as tourists and illegally work, study or even marry in the US. Innocent people tend to be victimised by summary removal proceedings when they make inconsistent statements, act nervously and are generally not sure of themselves.

I often find that the visa applicant lied when the truth would have worked. Don't try to be an expert, don't try to anticipate what the inspector or consular officer wants to hear. Just calmly tell the truth and you will find that you will have fewer problems at the airport and that government officials will be helpful. You will also save money on lawyers' fees.

CHANGE OF STATUS AND EXTENSION OF STAY

Once admitted to the US, a change in plans or employment may require an **extension of stay** or **change in visa status**. Provided that you did not violate the terms of your stay, you may extend the I-94 form or change immigration status while in the US. Applications for extensions or changes of status must be made through one of the USCIS Regional Processing Centers by filing appropriate forms and supporting documents. The USCIS must receive such petitions on or before the I-94 expiration date. Other than in exceptional circumstances, the USCIS denies I-94 extensions that are filed late. You may remain in the US during the process, even if the processing period extends beyond the I-94 validity date.

You may remain in the US if you extend your I-94 or change status on or before the I-94 expiration date. You may remain in the US for 120 days after the I-94 expiration date to wait for the USCIS response to your request for change of status or extension. Normally, 120 days suffice for USCIS processing.

Extensions require proof that you intend to stay in the US in the same employment capacity, and you must explain why you need the extension. The USCIS treats changes from one nonimmigrant status to another nonimmigrant status as a new petition. USCIS approval of an extension or change of status only permits you to remain in the US; you need a valid visa if you leave and wish to re-enter the country.

VISA REVALIDATION

As of July 2004, it is no longer possible to revalidate any
visa in the US. All visas must be obtained at an embassy or
consulate abroad.

NORTH AMERICAN FREE TRADE ACT VISAS

Canadians are visa-exempt except for **treaty trader** and
treaty investor visas which are controlled by a different
treaty from NAFTA. Canadians must file for treaty trader
or treaty investor visas at the US Consulate in Toronto.
Canadians must use the treaty trader or treaty investor visa
stamp to enter the US in that capacity.

Canadian tourists or business visitors do not need a visa
or prior USCIS approval to enter the US. In most other
cases, such as managers, professionals and treaty nationals
whose occupations are on the skills list, Canadians merely
present the USCIS approval letter at the border crossing.
The USCIS inspector will issue an I-94 to evidence the
correct status and stay period. No visa is required.

Canadians are supposed to be able to file and receive
one-day adjudication of visa petitions at border posts. The
system usually works but if the border officer chooses not
to make a decision, the application is forwarded to the
Nebraska Service Center, which holds jurisdiction for all
border crossings referrals.

SUMMARY

- A visa allows you to apply for entry to the US.
- Only the consuls issue visas.
- A single entry visa allows you to apply for entry one
  time within the visa validity period.
- A multiple entry permits you to apply for entry
  unlimited times within the visa validity period.
- You are applying for admission to the US when you

show your passport to the USCIS inspector at the airport or port of entry.

- The USCIS determines who comes into the USA and the length of stay.

- The I-94 card is evidence of how long you may stay in the US.

- Once you are inside the US, if you maintain legal status you may extend your stay or change to another visa status.

- If you leave the US you must have a valid visa to re-enter.

- Tell the truth to consuls and immigration inspectors and you will avoid summary removal proceedings. It's always better to tell the truth and return home rather than be barred from entry for five years.

BASIC CONCEPTS OF NONIMMIGRANT VISAS

The law creates two general types of visas: nonimmigrant and immigrant. A nonimmigrant visa terminates at a certain date. The immigrant visa holder may stay in the USA as long as he or she makes the US their permanent residence.

- With the exception of visa waiver countries, you need a visa in order to enter the United States for business or pleasure trips. If you plan to work in the US you need a visa regardless of how long you intend to remain. Visa waiver permits nationals of certain countries to enter the US for 90 days or less for business or tourist reasons. Most European countries and Japan qualify.

- The United States consulate or embassy located abroad issues all visas. USCIS may approve visa petitions, or requests for a visa, but USCIS does not issue visas. In most cases applicants must first obtain USCIS approval and then apply for a visa from the consulate.

Consulates may approve and issue B-1/B-2, E-1/2, I, R and a few other categories.

- To obtain USCIS visa approval file your petition with USCIS in the USA. Most petitions must be filed by mail or courier at one of four Regional Processing Centers. See Appendix 3.

- The USCIS will mail its decision as you instruct on the forms. If the USCIS approves your petition, take the approval notice, Form I-797, Form DS-156 (consular visa application form) and your passport to the US consulate that serves your area to apply for the visa. You must obtain visas outside the US.

- The consul may accept the USCIS decision, ask you for more information, interview you, or deny your visa application. The consuls have complete control over who receives visas. The consul may deny your visa application even if USCIS approved your petition. Normally the consul will issue visas according to the USCIS approval. The Consul places the visa stamp in your passport. The stamp shows place of issue, date of issue, number of permitted entries, duration, visa type, and if applicable the name of the US employer.

- Once you have your visa you may apply for entry to the US. The USCIS controls who enters the US just as the consuls control who receives visas. The USCIS may deny your entry to the US even if you have a valid visa. For example, if the USCIS inspector thinks a student is not really in school, he may deny entry. Often business cards to not match the employer noted under the visa stamp. The USCIS inspector may suspect you work for a different company from the one that applied for the visa. In such a case you may be denied entry.

- If the USCIS admits you to the US they will stamp Form I-94 Arrival Departure Card with the date of entry, visa type and expiration date. The aircraft crew hand out I-94 cards before landing. The dates on the I-94 card determine how long you may stay in the US.

- The dates on the I-94 card may be different from the dates on the visa. The I-94 card is evidence of how long you may stay in the US. You must leave the US or extend your I-94 by its expiration date, even if your visa is valid.

- With one exception, if the USCIS denies entry to the US you may either take the next flight home or ask for a hearing before an Immigration Judge. If you come to the US on visa waiver and the USCIS denies entry for any reason, you must leave. You have no right to a trial if you use visa waiver.

- It's always best to tell the truth to the consuls and to the Immigration Inspectors. If you tell the truth, they often try to help you. Most problems can be solved. If you lie nobody can help you. You can be barred from coming to the US for life if the consul or USCIS Inspector believes you committed fraud or materially misrepresented facts. Often, the truth would have worked. Don't try to be an expert, to anticipate what the Inspector or consular officer wants to hear. Calmly tell the truth and you will have fewer problems at the airport and government officials will be helpful. You will also save money on lawyers' fees.

3

Using a B-1 Visa

The **B-1 visa** permits business trips of less than six months' duration. The B-1 business visitor may not be employed in the US and must be paid from abroad. Because a visa waiver, if available, permits the same activities as the B-1, the B-1 visa is most often used for ongoing business, scientific or professional collaboration that takes more than 90 days to complete. Permissible activities include:

- business meetings

- scientific collaboration

- inspection of business opportunities

- meetings with government officials

- purchase of products

- negotiation of contracts

- selling products or services

- certain warranty or repair work.

With one exception B-1 visa holders may not work in the US. Foreign technicians may make warranty and repair service calls on B-1 visas within one year after the sale of the product, pursuant to a written purchase contract between the buyer and seller promising warranty and repair services.

APPLYING FOR ENTRY ON A B-1 VISA

To avoid problems at a port of entry B-1 visa holders should present documents that prove the purpose of their trip. Effective documentation may include:

- a copy of the warranty and repair contract if applicable
- an explanatory letter from the employer abroad
- a letter of invitation from the US business contacts
- a detailed itinerary.

You may also want to have somebody meet you at the airport to further explain the purpose of your trip or for language assistance.

WHAT CONSTITUTES WORK?

The primary purpose of the Immigration and Nationality Act is to protect US workers from cheap foreign labour. B-1 visa holders have the burden of convincing the USCIS inspector that they are spending up to six months in the US without working. Most people can't afford to spend six months at home without working, let alone in a foreign country. Because many B-1 holders were merely too lazy to get a proper working visa, the USCIS tends to be suspicious.

What constitutes work becomes an important question at a port of entry. Simply put, work means that your activity takes an American job. While it's clear that meetings, sales calls and scientific collaborations don't constitute work, the closer one gets to handling machinery, products or directing subordinate employees the harder it is to convince the USCIS inspector that you aren't working in the US.

Legally, B-1 visitors may handle equipment or products for demonstration purposes. This leaves the B-1 visitor with the problem of convincing the USCIS inspector that he only incidentally handles the product. Common sense dictates that the more time you spend in the US and the closer your activities come to handling products or machinery, the higher your burden of proof at a port of entry.

APPLICATION PROCEDURES AND STRATEGY

All nationalities except Canadians must apply for a B-1 visa at a US consulate. Provide the consular officer with background data to support the B-1 visa application. Important documentation includes:

- A detailed itinerary.

- Reasons for needing more than 90 days, if you are eligible for visa waiver, to conduct your business in the US.

- Proof that you will be paid from abroad.

- Proof that you are either an independent business person or that a foreign employer controls your activities.

Even if the consul issues the B-1 visa, you must still convince the USCIS inspector upon arrival in the US that you qualify for the B-1 visa at the time of entry. As in all visa matters, it's a two-step process: first you must make your case to the consul, after which you make your case to the USCIS inspector. You must pass both tests in order to enter the US.

Canadians merely state the purpose of their business trip at a port of entry. If the reasons are satisfactory, the inspector admits the Canadian without a B-1 visa or I-94 or other documentation. The maximum stay period is six months.

Assessing B-1 advantages

Because of uncertain results at US ports of entry I only recommend B-1 visas in special cases. Scientific collaborations, sales calls, work on a specific collaborative effort between a foreign and US company make good B-1 scenarios.

When in doubt try to obtain longer-term nonimmigrant working visas. B-1 visas often involve borderline situations where no clear definition of work exists. Most of us think we work when on a business trip. But you can't work while on a B-1 visa. It's easy to get confused and even easier for the USCIS to show you the door based on your confusion. Remember, USCIS can remove anybody they suspect of misrepresenting the purpose of their trip to the US without a hearing.

Although B-1 visa holders may avoid US income tax liability, it may be worth applying for a long-term working visa and paying the tax, to ensure that you can go about your business in the US without fear of immigration problems. The time, expense and disruption to your business resulting from being delayed or refused entry to the US may exceed the costs associated with a nonimmigrant working visa.

4

Travelling for Pleasure: The B–2 Visa

Since the advent of the visa waiver program, fewer people need **B-2 Visitor for Pleasure** visas. (Visa waivers are available for people from Canada, most European countries, and Japan.) After all, how many people take vacations that last more than two weeks, let alone more than the 90 days permitted under visa waiver? If you are eligible for a visa waiver, consuls usually will not issue a B-2 visa.

Normally, families or couples from non-visa waiver countries coming to the US for short vacations or even for a summer tour face few problems entering on visa waiver or obtaining B-2 visas. The B-2 application procedures are the same as for B-1 visas.

IDENTIFYING PROBLEM AREAS

Single young men and women and student-aged children face intense scrutiny when applying for a B-2 visa, or when applying for permission to enter the US. Student-aged children come to the US with or without parents, often posing as tourists, with the intention of enrolling in school. Mothers often stay in the US illegally to take care of the child. No visa category permits mothers to care for children going to American schools.

STUDENTS

If a child enters the US as a tourist without an endorsed visa, and later attempts to change to student status, the

USCIS may find that the child misrepresented his intentions for entering the US and deny the change of B-2 to F-1 student status request. Even if the USCIS approves the change of status from B-2 to F-1 student, and subsequently the student applies for a visa, most consuls will resist issuing an F-1 student visa for the same reasons. This will mean that the student cannot leave the US to apply for a visa with any assurance of being able to return. Students often find themselves 'locked' within the US, separated from their families, while holding a status for which they cannot get a visa.

Student-aged children intending to enrol in an American school should tell the consul the truth. If convinced of a child's student bonafides and financial support, the consul will issue a B-2 visa endorsed 'prospective student', or the like. Such an endorsement permits the children and parents to find a suitable school for the student. If all goes well the child may change to F-1 status while in the US, and later return home to apply for an F-1 student visa. Effective documentation for prospective F-1 students using a B-2 visa to shop for schools includes:

- academic references

- a list of prospective schools

- letters of invitation to visit schools

- proof of arrangements for care and support while attending school in the US.

YOUNG ADULTS

Young single men and women face a different problem. Many singles come to the US for no other purpose than to marry their way to a green card. The high incidence of singles coming to the US for this reason has influenced USCIS enforcement policy. Unfortunately, this policy creates difficulties for young singles who have legitimate reasons for visiting the US.

Yet there are ways for young singles to come to the US for legitimate travel reasons. It's important that they carefully document plans to return home following a vacation. Effective documentation includes:

- proof of a job or business at home

- proof of family ties at home (list family members)

- proof that you are pursuing an education at home

- a detailed itinerary of the US trip

- letters of invitation or reference from US citizens or permanent residents

- proof that you can support yourself while in the US.

In other words, provide proof that you have too much to lose by leaving home for an extended period.

5

Entering the US as a Fiancé(e)

Marriage to a US citizen qualifies you for a green card. If the marriage occurs abroad the green card petition must be filed through a US Consulate with jurisdiction over the applicant's place of residence. The procedures usually take between six to twelve months to complete depending on the country. Many newlyweds, for a variety of reasons, don't relish the idea of six months of separation or six months or so of waiting before they can enter the US as a married couple.

The same process that takes six to twelve months abroad also takes months in the US, but the applicant may work and live in the US from the date of filing. Those who apply abroad must wait outside the US during the entire processing period, unless they file for a K3 visa. K3 visas are discussed further in this chapter. As a result, many newlyweds prefer to undertake the entire green card application process in the US, so that they can live together and work while they patiently wait for the bureaucracy to grind out the green card approval notice.

The USCIS will not admit visitors who intend to live in the country permanently as a nonimmigrant. Your choices are to:

- apply abroad for a green card and come to the United States as a permanent resident

- enter the US using a K-1 (fiancé(e)) visa, or K-3 spousal visa

- or come to the United States as a nonimmigrant tourist or worker, then marry and apply for a green card.

In the latter case, if the USCIS knew all the facts they would deny entry and possibly bar entry for five years under summary removal procedures. One may not enter the US as a nonimmigrant with the intent to live in the US permanently.

THE FIANCÉ(E) VISA CATEGORY

Rather than force people to lie about the purpose of their entry to the US, in 1970 Congress created the K-1 or fiancé(e) visa category. The K-1 visa avoids the risk of being denied entry to the US or worse. The K-1 visa permits a fiancé(e) to enter the US as long as the marriage takes place within 90 days of entry. The visa may not be extended so be sure to marry within 90 days. The applicant may work in the US during the 90-day period. Immediately after the marriage, the couple may file the green card petition, Form I-130, and the adjustment of status petition I-485 with the USCIS. The K-1 visa tends to reduce the USCIS processing period because the K-1 visa application process requires much of the same information that the USCIS requires for the green card petition.

The K-3 visa was recently created for married persons overseas. A person married to a US citizen may now qualify for K-3 status to legally enter the US to adjust to permanent residence status rather than waiting abroad for the completion of the Embassy procedures. Married people may now adjust to permanent residence status abroad or in the US.

FOLLOWING PROCEDURES

The US citizen side of the equation files Form I-129F on behalf of the intended or spouse by mail at one of the four USCIS regional processing centres. This form requires personal data for each applicant, proof that the applicants have met within the two years prior to application and a statement that the applicants intend to marry within 90 days of entry to the US. The USCIS will make exceptions for arranged marriages if the applicants can show that arranged marriages are a family custom.

If the petition is approved, the USCIS will send the file to the Consulate nearest the residence of the alien fiancé(e) or spouse. The Consul will conduct security clearance procedures and then schedule an interview, much like a permanent residence interview. The applicant must supply pictures, a medical exam, and an affidavit of support. The green card interview and K-1 and K-3 interview procedures are almost identical.

If the Consul issues the visa, the supporting documents are put in a sealed envelope for presentation to the USCIS at the port of entry.

The fiancé(e) has four months from the date of visa petition approval to apply for the K-1 visa at a US Consulate. Although the four-month period may be extended, each extension request casts doubt on the ultimate intention to marry in the US.

The fiancé(e) must either marry within the 90-day period beginning with entry into the US or leave the US. If the fiancé(e) leaves prior to the expiration of the 90-day period and returns, he or she will only be admitted for the balance of the first 90-day period.

Fiancé(e) dependants receive a K-2 visa, which does not permit employment but does permit attending school.

The K-3 visa procedures are virtually identical to the K-1 visa with the following exceptions. First get married then file Form I-130 for immediate relative permanent residence status. When you receive the filing receipt from the USCIS, not the approval notice, you then file Form I-129F in Chicago. After issuance of the K-3 visa by the US Consulate the non-US spouse may enter the US. The non-US spouse may adjust status to permanent residence in the US (Form I-485) upon I-130 approval. The I-130 approval may arrive before or after the Consul issues the K-3 visa. In any event one must have I-130 approval before adjusting status to permanent residence. In short, the K-3 visa allows the applicant to enter the US as an intending permanent resident to complete the permanent residence procedures rather than waiting abroad to complete the procedures at the US Embassy.

SUMMARY

- The K-3 visa is the legal way for married persons to enter the US and complete their immigration procedures.

- Those who don't want to marry within 90 days need to use a B1/2 or nonimmigrant work visa and to hope that the USCIS inspectors don't ask the right question.

6

Temporary Working Visas

International organisations and corporations use nonimmigrant working visas to staff US operations. Investors use nonimmigrant visas for themselves and employees sent to the US to monitor investments. US employers use nonimmigrant visas to fill skill shortages in their companies. Many people use nonimmigrant working visas as a stepping stone to permanent residence status and then citizenship. People commonly obtain a nonimmigrant work visa so that they can remain in the US while applying or waiting for a green card.

This chapter defines the basic terms and concepts concerning the most commonly used nonimmigrant work visas: **E**, **H** and **L**. Subsequent chapters describe less frequently used categories along with the strategy and approach for specific situations.

GETTING THE GENERAL OUTLINE

The US maintains two interdependent nonimmigrant working visa systems. E visas are the product of treaties, negotiated between the US and other countries and administered by the Department of State through embassies and consulates. Congress created the other commonly used nonimmigrant work visas – H and L – through domestic law. The USCIS serves as the lead agency for administering H and L visas or other visas created by domestic law. Read this chapter before you read the chapters discussing how to staff companies, make investments in the US, or obtain a green card.

Most companies use a combination of E-1/2, H-1B, L-1A and L-1B visas to staff their US operations. The same person may qualify for an E visa category, or an H or L visa category. The combination of the H and L categories describes the same work activities as the E categories. E visas include professionals, managers, executives and essential skill employees, whereas H and L include professionals, executives, managers and specialised knowledge employees. Differences in corporate ownership and organisation, convenience, or the enforcement policies of the initial governmental agency you'll be working with, the USCIS or Department of State, determine whether to apply for an E visa or an H or L visa.

UNDERSTANDING THE TERMINOLOGY

Professionals
The term 'professional' refers to four-year university graduates who work in professional positions. These include lawyers, accountants, engineers, market researchers and economists. Depending on individual circumstances, a professional may quality for H-1B status, E status or even L-1A manager status.

Executive/manager
The term 'executive' is used literally. The term 'manager' refers to someone who directs or monitors the activities of other professionals, managers and supervisors. Managers are not involved in the direct manufacture of a product or provision of a service. Most executives and managers use E or L-1A manager visas.

International organisation
The term 'international organisation' refers to US companies having 50 per cent or more common ownership with a foreign company or individuals. Ownership may be traced through unlimited tiers of companies or individuals as long as one can ultimately establish 50 per cent or more common ownership.

Essential skill and specialised knowledge

'Essential skill' (E visa) or 'specialised knowledge' (L-1B visa) applicants possess knowledge critical to the success of the US (E visa) or beneficial to US competitiveness (L-1B visa).

When essential skills or specialised knowledge applicants also serve in executive/managerial or professional positions, they may also qualify for H-1B, L-1A or E visa status as professionals or executive managers.

L VISAS: INTRA-COMPANY TRANSFER

The L visa category includes executive, manager or specialised knowledge applicants who transfer within an international organisation. To qualify for any L category the visa applicant must transfer within the same international organisation. The applicant must work in a qualifying capacity (as an executive, manager or specialised knowledge employee) for a foreign member of the international organisation, for one of three years preceding the transfer to the American member of the international organisation in the same capacity. L visa applicants file Form I-129 and the L supplement with the USCIS.

As an example, a manager joined the foreign parent company in 1991 and resigned in June 1993. In June 1994 the foreign parent company rehired the manager to transfer to the US, then filed its L-1A petition. The manager meets the one-year test because he worked as a manager in the foreign parent company one of the three years prior to the petition filing date. If the applicant fails the one-year requirement, consider E or H-1B visa status.

To qualify as an international organisation the parent company must establish a branch office, subsidiary company or affiliate company in the US. From an immigration point of view, it makes little difference whether a branch, subsidiary or affiliated company is formed as long as the arrangement qualifies as an international organisation for L-1 purposes. International organisations are as follows.

Branch office in the US
A branch office refers to the parent company registering itself to do business in the US, as opposed to forming a subsidiary or affiliate.

Subsidiary company
A subsidiary for L visa purposes is a US company owned 50 per cent or more by a foreign corporation.

Affiliated company
An affiliated company is a business linked by at least 50 per cent common ownership to the foreign parent. For L-1 purposes the foreign parent must directly or indirectly control the US branch, subsidiary or affiliate. Control in this case generally means 50 per cent or more direct or indirect ownership.

A 50-50 joint venture between a foreign and American company may be an affiliate of the foreign company since the foreign company owns half of the US business. The joint venture could be a partnership between the US company and the foreign company's wholly-owned US subsidiary. Or it could be a corporation owned half by US shareholders or companies, and half by the foreign company or its subsidiary. Many foreign companies transfer managers, executives or specialised knowledge persons to US joint-venture operations.

TREATY TRADER/INVESTOR BASIC TERMINOLOGY

The following discussion involves the workings of the treaty trader/investor treaties. It's difficult to understand how to use E visa without some background on the subject.

The E categories include executives, managers, professional and essential skill applicants hired by a company controlled by at least 50 per cent of the treaty nationals involved in qualifying trade or investment. The E visa applicant must be of the same nationality as the controlling ownership. The American E visa employer qualifies as a treaty company on the basis of the nationality of its shareholders as well as the qualifying trade or investment.

E visa employees – E visa employees must be of the same nationality as the E visa company. If the E visa company is owned by 50 per cent or more UK shareholders the E visa employees must be UK citizens. The E visa employee does not need to be a prior employee of the E visa company in the UK, any qualifying UK national will do.

E visa applicants must take an active role in the enterprise. Mere passive ownership will not qualify for E visa status. For example: Hands on managers, professionals and persons with special skills qualify. A purely passive shareholder with no executive or managerial responsibilities will not qualify. An executive who oversees general affairs but does not participate in the daily operations of the company qualifies. A company Director with no other responsibilities will not qualify.

The US does not offer a retirement visa. People often structure an investment for E visa purposes that also serves retirement goals. One could call executive supervision over substantial real estate holdings semi-retirement or even full retirement depending on one's point of view. The closest visa to an outright retirement visa is the permanent residence category for immigrant investors discussed in detail in the chapter titled 'Five Ways to Obtain a Green Card'.

E visa processing

E visa processing consists of two basic steps. First, the US company must be qualified as a **Treaty Trader** or **Treaty Investor**. The US company must prove it made a substantial investment or controls substantial qualifying trade. Secondly, the company must prove the applicant qualifies as an executive, manager or essential skill employee.

The applicant, if in the US, may change to E status by filing for an USCIS change of status on Form I-129,

Application for Nonimmigrant Workers, with the E supplement. If the applicant works abroad the application must be filed with a consul. Forms, procedures and enforcement policies vary among the consular offices.

The treaty national employees of a treaty trader company receive E-1 visas. The treaty national employees of a treaty investor company obtain E-2 visas. When the same company qualifies for both E-1 and E-2 status, the consul will only accord the applicant one status. For example, the United Kingdom is a 'treaty country', thus making a UK-controlled company in the US a 'treaty company' and a UK citizen working for the treaty company a 'treaty national'.

The treaties

The 'treaty' refers to a **Friendship Commerce and Navigation Treaty (FCN)** or a **Bilateral Investment Treaty (BIT)** between the US and a foreign country. Such treaties contain agreements concerning trade, investing, shipping, aviation and staffing of operations in each country. The US has negotiated such treaties with over 50 countries, including Japan, Taiwan, Korea, Thailand, most European countries and Canada.

The US originally negotiated FCN and BIT treaties to assure equal access to foreign markets and prevent arbitrary limitations on the number of treaty nationals permitted to staff foreign operations. Now that the US runs a trade deficit, FCN and BIT treaties tend to protect foreign nationals doing business in the US. Twenty-five years ago, the reverse was true.

Many countries created arbitrary ratios (such as one American technician per five Japanese technicians) to assure local control of foreign enterprises. FCN and BIT treaties prevented this practice by giving treaty traders or investors the opportunity to staff foreign operations with qualified persons of their 'choice'.

Although there is no legal limit on the number of E visa employees, over the years the State Department limited the treaty company's 'choice' by imposing training requirements, suggesting that treaty companies hire more US workers, or by strictly defining the classes of eligible workers. Today, 'choice' means that the treaty company may employ as many applicants as it wants as long as the consul agrees.

CONTROL AND OWNERSHIP OF A US TREATY COMPANY

'Control' refers to 50 per cent or more treaty national ownership of a US company. Japan is a treaty country, and a joint venture based in the US and controlled by 50 per cent or more of Japanese treaty nationals qualifies as a treaty company. US subsidiaries of companies such as Sony and Honda are treaty companies. Public companies generally take the nationality of their primary place of incorporation or the location of the stock exchange that trades most of their shares.

Subsequent changes in corporate ownership by either the parent or US treaty company may affect treaty status. Treaty nationals must at all times control the US treaty company. If at any time treaty national ownership dips below 50 per cent, the US treaty company loses its treaty status. Fifty-fifty joint ventures risk losing treaty status if US shareholders purchase additional shares from the treaty national shareholders, thus changing the ownership ratio.

Note that green card holders count as US workers for E visa purposes regardless of their nationality. In the above example, a UK green card holder does not qualify as a treaty national as he or she is considered a 'US person.'

TREATY TRADER: E-1 VISA

Service and trading companies may qualify for E-1 treaty trader status. 'Trade' signifies trade in goods and trade in services. Banks, financial service companies, software firms, attorneys, accountants and the like, along with companies trading goods, may qualify for E-1 treaty trader status.

Treaty trade means substantial trade primarily between the treaty national countries. 'Primarily' means that 50 per cent or more of the treaty company trade (the US operation) is between the treaty company and the treaty country. If Honda USA wants to be a treaty trader company, over half of its imports and exports must be between the US and Japan.

Treaty trade must be substantial, though there is no specific monetary amount to define 'substantial'. Enforcement varies among US consuls world-wide as local economic conditions dictate the definition of substantial treaty trade.

In Japan, Taiwan, Korea and Europe, substantial trade generally involves many small annual transactions of at least $500,000, or a few large annual transactions in the millions of dollars. In lesser developed countries, consuls often approve E-1 visas for smaller amounts of trade. Generally, the poorer the country the lower the trade threshold. Consuls focus on business activity and try to limit treaty trader status to active and on-going business ventures, not short-term projects.

Direct trade

Only direct trade qualifies for E-1 purposes. For example, US-incorporated Japanese treaty Company A sells to US-incorporated UK treaty Company B. Company B exports to the UK. Company A cannot claim B's exports for E-1 trade purposes even if the British buyer is A's parent company. If Company A wants E-1 status, it must make sure the exports are shipped under its name.

Trade primarily between the US and a treaty country

Trade between the US and a treaty country must exceed 50 per cent of the US treaty company's total world-wide trade. 'Trade' is defined by the US treaty company's commerce with a treaty country. In one case, a Taiwanese company exports from the US to Taiwan through a branch office in America. As the US dollar lost value, trade between the US and Taiwan fell to less than 50 per cent of the company's total trade. Because of this drop in trade the company lost its E-1 visa status.

Doing business in the US through a US-incorporated subsidiary prevents the above scenario. A branch office is part of the parent company, not a separate company. Thus the parent is also the treaty company. A branch office must compare its trade with the treaty country to the parent company's total world-wide trade. A US subsidiary is a separate company, not part of the parent company. In the case of a subsidiary company, 'treaty trade' refers to the subsidiary company's trade with the treaty country. As long as the US subsidiary does 50 per cent or more of its import/export business with the treaty country (not necessarily the parent company), the trade will be primarily between the US and the treaty country.

TREATY INVESTOR E-2

E-2 status requires a substantial treaty investment. A 'substantial investment' in a business generally involves at least $200,000. Payment may be in cash or a combination of cash and debt. Depending on national conditions and individual circumstances, the US Consulate may approve cases for smaller ventures. Although there is no statutory minimum investment, the smaller the investment the tougher it is to get visa approval. Funds must come from the treaty country of the investor, and borrowed funds may not be secured by assets of the treaty investment.

The smaller the cost of the business the higher the percentage of cash investment required. Consular officers usually require a cash investment of 65 per cent, or $130,000, for a business that costs $200,000. A million-dollar investment requires a smaller investment percentage. Again, these are only general guidelines. Consuls base their decisions on the specific facts of each case.

BASIC REQUIREMENTS OF H-1B VISAS: FOR PROFESSIONAL WORKERS

The applicant must have professional qualifications and work in a job requiring these qualifications. For example, a staff economist should have a Bachelor of Arts degree in Economics. The term 'speciality worker' used in the regulations really means 'professional worker'. If the applicant does not have a university degree, it's best to find an alternative visa status. The regulations may exempt people with twelve or more years of work experience from the degree requirement. However, if there's another visa choice, use it. Qualifying for H-1B status without a university degree is very difficult and requires a credentials evaluation.

The US government limited the number of H-1B visas to 195,000 per year until 30 September 2003. Until 1998 the quota was 55,000. The increase in usage comes primarily from the high-tech industries. Because the size of the quota is a hotly debated polical issue, one cannot predict the size of future quotas.As this goes to press, all allotted H-1 visas for US fiscal year 2006 are used, excepting a few remaining for those who earned a master's degree in the US.

As long as computer and biotech continue to grow the quota will probably continue to be insufficient. Those who can plan ahead should file as close as possible to the beginning of the government fiscal year, 1 October.

In order to win passage of the legislation to increase the quota, organised labour demanded an additional filing fee to pay for worker training and scholarships. This additional fee is due for all initial H-1B petitions, the first extension, any change of employer. All companies except educational institutions and non-profit companies must pay the additional filing fee. The additional filing fees are $750 if the US company, and any US subsidiaries or affiliates, have 25 or less employees. If more than 25 employees, the filing fee becomes $1500. There is also a $500 fraud fee for first applications and any change of employer.

H-1B employers

H-1B employers may be completely US owned, completely foreign owned, or a combination of the two. An H-1B employer must be incorporated or otherwise licensed to do business in the US, *ie* an American employer. An American employer, or a US agent of a foreign employer, must petition for H-1B and L status. Foreign employers may petition for E status. The term 'US employer' refers to the place of incorporation or licensure, not ownership. A totally foreign owned US corporation is a US employer because it is incorporated in the US.

The Labor Conditions Application process

H-1B employers must file a Labor Conditions Application (LCA) form with the US Department of Labor, post the form on the company bulletin board for ten days, or give the form to a union representative prior to filing for H-1B. The LCA form requires the employer to disclose the H-1B applicant's job title and salary to ensure there is no labour problem, and to promise to pay the H-1B applicant the prevailing wage. Only after LCA certification may employers petition the USCIS for H-1B status. Allow 90 days for H-1B processing.

'Prevailing wage' is the salary that the Department of Labor determines most people in the work area earn for a particular job. Employers must document how they determined the prevailing wage. It's best to obtain a prevailing wage determination from the State Department of Labor before filing an H-1B petition. American companies looking for low-priced foreign labour often have trouble with the prevailing wage rate.

Many companies resist telling US workers the salary of a new foreign worker. However, the Department of Labor may levy fines and/or prohibit the employer from applying for H-1B visas for not posting the LCA notice where all employees can see it, failing to disclose accurate information, or not paying the prevailing wage.

'Dependent employers', or companies of 50 or more employees with 15 per cent or more foreign workers, in addition to meeting the prevailing wage standards must attest that they recruited for the position prior to hiring the H-1B worker and offered the position to equally or more qualified US workers, and that the employer has not laid off a US worker in the same position as the intended H-1B within 90 days before and after filing the H-1B petition.

There is a sliding scale for smaller companies.

'Dependent employers' also include companies with one to 25 total employees with nine or more H-1B employees and companies with 12–25 total employees with 14 or more H-1B employees. The 'dependent employers' attestation, although difficult to enforce, gives the Department of Labor an additional lever to discourage the use of foreign labour.

The H-1B attestation requirements are unavoidable, the only alternative being to use another visa category. However, you don't always have that choice.

PROFESSIONAL LICENCES

H-1B professionals must either be licensed in the state of intended employment or be exempt from the licence requirement. State law defines the professions which require a licence. In most cases, professionals such as engineers, lawyers, accountants or architects, who work for a company and do not serve the public, don't require state licences. One must consult state law to determine licence requirements.

As an example, companies often transfer a person to oversee the legal matters of their US operations. In many countries, universities offer an undergraduate programme in commercial law. Commonly, graduates never take a bar exam or obtain a licence to practise law. In-house lawyers or businessmen with law degrees qualify for H-1B status.

The typical applicant usually holds a commercial law degree and has worked with the company's benefit programmes, labour relations, regulatory compliance, or contractual negotiations. The applicant never took a licence to practise law. The applicant will be transferred to the US subsidiary to coordinate subsidiary and home-office legal affairs, monitor regulatory compliance, engage outside professionals on an as-needed basis, coordinate home-office and subsidiary benefit plans, and monitor compliance with US civil rights anti-discrimination rules. This applicant doesn't need a licence to practise law because he serves his company, not the public.

H-1B Portability Rules

H-1B visas are only valid for work for the petitioning employer and are only valid for six years. There are two exceptions to the general rule. An H-1B employee may change jobs and work for the new employer using the old H-1B visa once the new H-1B petition has been filed. The applicant may work for the new employer from the time of filing the new petition without waiting for USCIS approval. Initial H-1B applicants must wait for visa approval to commence employment.

Employees who have applied for labour certification before the end of their 5 th year of H-l status, or, if the labour certification is approved, but the visa numbers have regressed may extend their H-1B visas in one-year increments beyond the six-year limit.

Pointers for individuals using H-1B professional status to work in the US

- You must arrange a job with a definite offer of employment before applying for the H-1B visa.

- Although you may apply from abroad, you need the job offer first.

- Lawyers generally can't help you find a job. Find a job first, then call the lawyer to help with the visa process.

- Negotiate an employment contract. H-1B employers must pay your airfare home if you get fired.

- H-1B visas only last six years. Make sure you have enough time (allow two years to be safe) to obtain a green card before the H-1B validity period terminates.

- Professional and scientific university degrees make for an easier case than liberal arts degrees.

- Young, inexperienced applicants must convince the consular officer that the job is *bona fide*, not an accommodation to the applicant.

- Currently, H-1B visas are subject to an annual quota of 65,000, which does not suffice for demand. If the numbers are gone, it is best to apply as soon as possible for the coming fiscal year, which is October 1. Regulations allow applying for H-1B's six months in advance of the start date, or April 1.

Pointers for employers using H-1B visas for professional workers

- You must pay the prevailing wage. The trend is towards higher prevailing wages, hence there is a temptation to cheat. Don't do it!

- If the state job service prevailing wage is too high, you may rely on private employment surveys. Although the Department of Labor must accept private surveys, the best proof that you paid the prevailing wage is a certification from the state job service. Private surveys save time and you eliminate dealing with the state job service, but they don't afford the best protection against complaints from US workers that you paid a foreigner less than the prevailing wage. On the other hand, it's often your only choice, because state job services frequently believe the prevailing wages are higher than the wage you would be willing to pay.

- Young H-1B employees with little working experience often ultimately want a green card. Because they can't count experience gained with the petitioning employer (see Chapter 9 on labour certification), they must find a different employer for the green card process. You may invest in an employee only to lose him later. Investigate an employee's desire for a green card and the likelihood for success before you make the hire.

- Your prospective H-1B employee may be in the US on a tourist or student visa. Don't hire the H-1B employee until the H-1B visa is approved, unless the employee has a different visa permitting him to work for your company. Allow 120 days for H-1B visa processing.

- Remember the additional filing fees. The additional fees are either $750 or $1500, depending upon the total number of employees, plus the $500 fraud fee

- Although part-time employment is permitted, employers must state their intention to hire the employee part-time on the application form.

KNOWING WHEN TO USE H, L OR E

Corporate organisation, convenience, or the applicant's background may dictate whether to apply for E, H or L categories. Each of the E, H and L categories permits the applicant to work in the US and allows spouses and dependent children to live or study in the US. E and L spouses, not dependents, may file form I-765 upon arrival in the US for work authorization. H visa spouses and children may not work in the US. Dependent children must be under age 21. Children over 21 need an independent visa status. All three categories are employer-specific. The holder of the visa may only work for the sponsoring employer.

Assuming you may choose between E, H or L status, consider the following guidelines:

- E visas may be extended as long as the US business remains viable. There is no limit to extensions of the visa. Most consuls issue E visas for five-year periods.

- L visas are limited to seven years for executives and managers and five years for specialised knowledge. H visas are limited to six years for professionals. Most initial L-1 and H-1B visas are valid for three years.

- If you ultimately want a green card, try to arrange your affairs so that you are transferred in a managerial or executive capacity within an international organisation.

- If none of the above matters to you, apply for the category that affords the fastest and easiest processing. This depends on a comparison of the enforcement policies and service standards of the consulate nearest

your home to those of the USCIS service centre
controlling the area of your intended employment.

SUMMARISING ELIGIBILITY FOR E, H AND L VISA HOLDERS

L visas accommodate transfers within an international
organisation, and E visas accommodate citizens or
companies of the treaty country involved in qualifying trade
or investment. H-1B professionals may work for any
incorporated or licensed US company that requires the
services of a professional. The definitions overlap and the
same person may qualify for one or more visa categories.

The following scenarios clarify company requirements for
the E, H and L visas. If the US employer is:

- A member of an L visa international organisation and
  qualifies for either E-1 or E-2 status, the company may
  use L, H and E visas.

- Not a member of an L visa international organisation but
  qualifies for either E-1 or E-2 status, the company may
  use E or H visas.

- Not a member of an L visa international organisation,
  and does not qualify for E-1 or E-2 status, the company
  may only use H visas.

In rare cases, consider O, P and Q visas. See Chapter 11.

Pay to Play
Due to complaints about slow processing times, the USCIS
initiated expedited processing fees. One can pay an
additional $1,000 along with Form I-907 to obtain 15-day
processing service. The USCIS promises an answer, not
necessarily a decision within 15 days of receipt of the
petition. An 'answer' may merely be a request for more
information. Expedited processing is now available for most
H and L category visa petitions, and for Es filed in the US
as either change of status or extension of status. There is no
premium processing at embassies or consulates.

7

Sending Staff to a New Business in America

Typically clients come to my office and say, 'I want to open my business in America. How do I do it?' At this point there is usually no more than an idea or business plan to work with.

ESTABLISHING THE US COMPANY FIRST

No matter what visa alternative you ultimately choose you will need to establish a US company licensed to do business in a particular state. The USCIS will not consider most business oriented visa petitions unless a US company exists. Although there are reasons to establish partnerships, joint ventures or even to use individual ownership, in most cases it's best to form a limited company or a corporation.

The USCIS is familiar with corporations. It is not familiar with limited partnerships, complicated general partnerships, and limited liability companies. If you can help it, don't complicate your petition.

Simply put, shareholders of corporations only risk their capital in the company. Partners or sole proprietors place all their assets at risk in the event of a law suit or business failure. Limited liability companies, Sub S corporations and limited partnerships are hybrids between corporate and individual ownership.

Considering death taxes
Although a discussion of the tax advantages and disadvantages of the various forms of ownership is beyond

the scope of this book, a short explanation of death taxes is in order. The US levies estate or death tax upon the death of a US tax resident. US tax residents include some nonimmigrants, permanent residents and citizens. The estate tax on nonimmigrants and permanent residents is much higher than the estate tax on citizens.

Corporations have eternal life. Individual shareholders will die but not the corporation. A corporation owned by a foreign corporation doesn't even have a shareholder that can die. If there's no death there's no estate tax. Using a foreign corporation to own the shares of the US corporation not only works best for most immigration purposes, but also offers the possibility of reducing estate taxes.

FORMING THE CORPORATION

Incorporating a company in the US is a simple matter; there is no federal or national registration. Incorporate at the state level, not with the federal government in Washington D.C. Most states use similar rules and procedures. No states conduct background checks, limit entry into particular businesses or require a minimum amount of capital.

Most European and Asian countries require maintenance of a minimum amount of capital in return for granting the shareholders the rights of limited liability. The US grants corporate shareholders limited liability free of charge.

Foreigners may serve as officers or directors without restriction. Officers and directors do not have to reside in the state of incorporation or in the US.

Additionally, apply for a tax identification number as well as state and local business licences. Accountants normally take care of the initial registrations. Normally, processing takes a matter of a few weeks. Corporate filing fees vary from state to state; most states charge under $1,000. You can incorporate without the services of an attorney, but it's usually not worth the time and risk of undertaking an unfamiliar task to save $1,000 or so in attorney fees.

FINDING PREMISES FOR DOING BUSINESS

There's no choice; the USCIS will also not consider business oriented petitions without proof of a place to do business. Don't use an apartment or residence.

APPLYING FOR THE WORKING VISA

Once the office and the company is established you may apply for your working visa. Most people apply for either L-1A international manager, E1/2 treaty trader or investor, or H-1B speciality occupations.

Most companies apply for L-1A visas because this category was designed to accommodate start-up companies. The L-1A permits a manager to come to the US for an initial one-year period to establish the enterprise. E1/12 visas require existing trade or investment irrevocably committed to the enterprise. The H-1B was not designed for start-ups but can be used at a pinch. The L-1A requires a company licence, secured premises, a reasonable business plan and proof of the ability to execute the business plan.

The foreign parent company must prove that it has sufficient capital and experience to support the fledgling US business. The visa applicant must be a managerial or executive employee who worked for the corporate group for one of the three years prior to the petition date.

CASE STUDY

A foreign chemical company plans to enter the US market. It already sells products through a US distributor, and wants to establish a US subsidiary to ultimately purchase the distributor, and establish sales and manufacturing operations in the US.

The transfer candidate, a 35-year-old manager with ten years' experience with the parent company, will be the only employee during the start-up period. The candidate manages export sales to the US for the parent company, and has worked with the US distributor. While working in the US the candidate will conduct market research and prepare for the takeover of the distributor. The foreign company leases office space from the distributor and has established a US subsidiary corporation.

This should be a textbook case of proper eligibility for the L-1A visa category. There are a US company, a parent company with money and experience, a leased office and a verifiable business plan. Even though the foreign company was a multi-billion dollar company, the USCIS questioned the petitioner's ability to carry out the business plan. We pointed out that the parent company, a multi-national corporation, had more than sufficient cash, savings and experience to open a new branch office and the petition was approved.

Learning some lessons

There are two lessons to be learned. The people adjudicating petitions for the USCIS are often inexperienced, poorly trained and never have enough time to thoroughly read the file. Hence the USCIS often asks for information they already have, and many of the USCIS requests for further information are generated from a word processor and have nothing to do with the instant file. Rather than getting upset, it's best to give the USCIS what they want, even if that means sending the same document again and pointing out that it was already in the file.

The other lesson to be learned is that the USCIS scrutinises applications involving start-up companies because start-ups often don't make it and are often established for the primary purpose of obtaining a green card, rather than for a business purpose. There's an easy solution to this problem: send money. Send enough money to the new US company to cover operations for a year. Also supply a detailed budget of the first two or three years' operations, showing where the money comes from. Although the L-1A category does not require a specific amount of initial capital, applicants must prove the ability to sustain the company during the first year of operations. Put another way, you need to pay to play.

EXPLORING ALTERNATIVES TO THE L-1A APPROACH

Using the E1/2 visa

The parent company could have capitalised the US subsidiary and signed a purchase and sale agreement to purchase the US distributor. Depending on the amount, the capital transfer, coupled with the purchase and sale agreement and the existing trade between the parent company and the US, should permit one E1 or E2 manager, assuming the appropriate treaty nationality, to come to the US to establish the subsidiary company.

The E1/2 visa alternative must be considered when the managerial transferee does not have one year's managerial experience abroad as required for the L-1A visa. Because the E1/2 visa categories were designed to accommodate existing trade or investment, the petition must demonstrate a higher showing of commitment of capital or existence of trade than in the case of the L-1A visa.

Using the example above, the L-1A visa application does not require a commitment to purchase the US distributor. The E visa petition either requires proof of existing trade or proof of a contract, backed with at least a deposit, to purchase the US distributor.

The H-1B visa offers an interesting alternative to the L-1A visa for start-up companies. Employees with a professional level of education, Baccalaureate degree or better, who come to work in a professional position for US employers, qualify for H-1B status.

Using the H-1B visa

An overview of the H-1B regulations suggests that the US employer is an existing and active business with other US employees. On the other hand the regulations merely state that the employer must be a US employer. A US employer is any company formed and licensed to do business in the US, regardless of ownership. Thus the start-up company described in the above example qualifies as a US employer. Until the USCIS changes the rules, H-1B visas are viable in start-up company situations.

The first person to staff the start-up usually conducts market research and formulates the plan for launching the business. Depending upon the scope of the project, market research often requires professional expertise. Bachelor of Arts degrees in marketing, business, commercial law, economics, political science, accounting and finance logically support business planning or market research positions. In technical areas, market research may require an engineering or other scientific degree.

The H-1B visa provides two advantages over L-1A in the start-up situation. The USCIS usually issues the initial H-1B visa for three years, not an initial one-year period as in the L-1A, and there is no requirement to hire employees as in the case of the L-1A. On the down side, the H-1B filing fee can be as much as $1,500 higher than the L-1A filing fee and a corporate officer will have to sign the H-1B labour conditions attestation forms.

MAKING THE FINAL CHOICE

The L-1A is the preferred method for new companies because the regulations specifically accommodate start-up companies. Furthermore, it may be easier to obtain a green card starting from L-1A status. The H-1B is a last resort to be considered after L-1A and E1/2 visa alternatives.

EXTENDING YOUR US STAY AFTER THE ONE YEAR PERIOD

Start-up company L-1A visas have an initial validity period of one year, not three years as in other L-1A situations. The L-1A manager must conduct active business and hire employees within the one-year period. Remember, L-1A managers must oversee other managers, supervisors or professionals. At a minimum, the manager must make tangible progress towards establishing the business. At the end of the first year the L-1A visa can be extended for up to two three-year periods.

H-1B visa holders are limited to six consecutive years in the US. The L-1A visa holders are restricted to seven consecutive years in the US. At the end of the maximum validity period they may change to any other status than H-1B or L-1A, often E1/2, or they must leave the US for at least one year before reapplying in H-1B or L-1A status.

L-1A visa renewals become difficult unless the manager makes tangible progress in establishing an active US business. Tangible progress includes:

- hiring two or three people

- showing a trend of increasing gross sales

- acquisition of necessary capital assets; or

- construction/remodel of premises or a factory.

Larger companies fare better in this regard as they can say their lack of progress is due to bigger projects which take more time to launch. They can easily prove they have the capital necessary to continue the project. Small companies have more difficulty and may decide to use H-1 status instead or change to H-1B status. E1/2 visa will not work without active trade or a substantial investment.

Understanding the one year rule

The USCIS designed the one-year 'doing business' requirement to force the applicant company to show good faith in efforts to establish itself in the US. In the 1980s many Taiwanese companies established US subsidiary 'shell' companies as a vehicle to move children to the US to study and to later apply for a green card. The USCIS established the one-year doing business rule for start-up companies to curtail this abuse.

Russian and PRC Chinese companies tend to follow the trail blazed by their Taiwanese predecessors. The USCIS tends to not only question Russian and PRC Chinese start-up company applications, but often sends the files to field investigators who visit the premises in the home country and the US to check the bona-fides of the visa petition. This practice not only delays processing but also creates some unfortunate results. We have had to appeal several cases where the USCIS checked the wrong address or the manager was simply out of the office when the USCIS investigator knocked on the door.

Technically, the USCIS must consider mitigating circumstances when determining compliance with the one year of doing business rule. Reasonable excuses include bad luck, unforeseen delays, and the fact that some businesses take longer to establish than others. The USCIS tends to take a harsh and simplistic view. If after one year there are no new employees and no trend of increasing gross sales, no visa extension will be issued.

PASSING THE ONE YEAR OF BUSINESS HURDLE

With an extended L-1A visa safely in hand the employer must decide what to do at the end of the seven-year maximum L-1A validity period. There are three reasonable choices:

1. Rotate L-1A managers. Continue using L-1A visas for successor managers.

2. If eligible change to E1/2 visa at the end of the maximum validity period. The E1/2 has no maximum validity period.

3. Apply for a green card after one year of doing business in the US. See Chapter 9.

WHAT ABOUT THE CHILDREN?

Children fall under the principal applicant's visa status until the age of 21. Spouses and children receive H-4 or L-2 visas. E visa dependants receive the same designation as the principal alien endorsed as the dependant. Children may not work in the US without a visa that specifically authorises employment. Dependent status does not authorise employment. After age 21, children must obtain independent immigration status. E and L spouses, not dependents, may file form I-765 upon arrival in the US for work authorisation. H visa spouses and children may not work in the US.

Many dependants are in university at the time they turn 21 years of age and may qualify for F-1 student status. Children with an F-1 student visa, with few exceptions, cannot work except for a one-year period of practical training. At some point the child will graduate. At that time, adult children must change from F-1 to another visa category, or return home.

Getting a visa of their own

Dependants over 21 years of age cannot work or stay in the US for the long term without getting married to a US citizen, or finding a job that leads to a visa. Most university graduates, if they can find a job requiring a university degree, will qualify for H-1B status. The H-1B visa holder must go through labour certification to qualify for a green card (see Chapter 9). This can be a lengthy process and it is always costly.

Marriage of convenience is out of the question. First of all it is illegal. Then consider the fact that the foreign spouse is hostage to the US spouse until the green card arrives and possibly after. Those who are found out can be prohibited from coming to the US forever. As in most things, life is tough but it's tougher if you are stupid.

As a result, some parents obtain green cards before the children reach 21. The green card petition includes children under the age of 21. A green card permits children to remain in the US without parents, and to freely study and work in the US. State universities treat green card holders as residents eligible for the less costly resident tuition.

EXPLORING THE ALTERNATIVES

As you can see, there are several viable approaches to staffing a new company in the US. In most cases, you will choose the L-1A visa, but there are good reasons to explore the other alternatives.

8

Staffing an Existing US Business

Now that we have described how to staff a start-up enterprise, let's look at staffing existing businesses. This chapter discusses:

- Treaty trader or treaty investor E-1 and E-2

- L-1A Manager

- L-1B Specialised Knowledge

- H-1B Professional Visas

- H-2B Seasonal Workers or Labor Unavailable in the US.

CHOOSING THE CORRECT VISA

Each visa category presents advantages and disadvantages. Consuls generally process E visa petitions faster than the USCIS processes H and L visa petitions. L-1A visas work better than other categories in start-up situations. H-1B petitions require LCA disclosures. The LCA disclosure entails additional processing time and may disturb relations with US workers. L-1B visas tend to require detailed explanations of the applicant's benefit to US competitiveness, while L-1A visas tend to require detailed explanations of the company's organisation and the applicant's managerial duties.

The E-1/2 essential skill category requires the US company to train replacements. The H-2B category requires recruitment of US workers. H and L visas have maximum validity periods, while E visas may be extended indefinitely. On the other hand, H-1B, L-1A, L-1B and E visas all permit

the applicant to work in the US while allowing dependants to
live and attend school in America.

MANAGERS

Most L-1A or E manager petitions are straightforward.
Companies hire an endless variety of managers and
executives, including administrative managers, human
resource managers, accounting managers, production
managers, company officers, sales managers, *etc.* Simply put,
managers tell other managers, supervisors and professionals
what to do.

Problems arise when the so-called manager is actually a
front line supervisor. Front line supervisors do not manage
other managers, supervisors or professionals. The USCIS
often questions petitions for production managers, sales
managers and other positions that are often non-managerial.
In such cases be prepared to furnish detailed organisational
charts of the position abroad and the proposed position in the
US as well as payroll records.

Managers and executives working for an international
organisation may qualify for L-1A Manager, E-1/2 Manager,
or H-1B Manager serving in a professional capacity.
Managers working for a treaty company that isn't part of an
international organisation qualify for E-1/2 or H-1B. If the
company isn't a treaty organisation or an international
organisation, H-1B Professional status becomes the only
choice. Treaty organisations or international organisations
may pay managers from abroad. In such cases the US
employer must remit payroll tax and income tax withholding
to the IRS for wages earned in the US.

Managers may commute between foreign and American
locations. If questioned, the manager must demonstrate that
he performs managerial duties while in the US. It's not how
much time the manager spends in the US, it's what the
manager does while there.

Corporate organisation will either expand or limit your
choices. Assuming you have all three choices – H-1B, L-1A
and E-1/2 – consider the following points:

Factors favouring E visas

- In most cases, consuls process visas faster than the USCIS.

- E visa holders receive up to two-year stay periods every time they enter the US. An E visa holder entering the US on the last day of his visa may be admitted for up to two years beyond the visa expiration date. This, however, may change.

- L or H visa holders will only be admitted for a period not longer than their visa validity date. Depending on the circumstances, the E visa may eliminate the need to file an extention petition with the USCIS.

- The E visa may theoretically be extended indefinitely, whereas the H visa is limited to six years unless pending labour certification, and the L-1A visa is limited to seven years.

- If the company is replacing an E visa holder with a person serving the same position, use the E visa category for the replacement. By granting the E visa the first time the consul has already determined that the position qualifies.

Factors favouring H and L visas

- Consuls usually review the US employer's staffing history. Consuls generally resist granting E visas for more than one person per position. The USCIS only reviews the case in front of them, and usually doesn't review the entire company's staffing structure and visa history. For example, if you think there will be trouble justifying the need for more than one sales manager, use the L-1A or H-1B categories.

- Consuls tend to question E visa petitions for managers under 30 years of age. In such cases, if the manager also has a professional degree consider H-1B or L-1A.

- If your company frequently uses E visas and cannot demonstrate a declining ratio of foreign versus American workers, consider H and L visas for new positions.

Determining the correct visa is more of an art than a science. One must consider long-term staffing goals. If your company plans to rotate managers between the US and foreign offices, it's important to establish precedents with the USCIS and consuls for all possible categories.

If hiring a foreign manager is an infrequent or one-time situation, use the visa category that best suits the applicant's credentials and long-term goals. For example, if the applicant may ultimately want a green card and the US employer is part of an international organisation, use the E or L-1A categories. As you will see in the next chapter, changing to a green card from an H-1B visa can be difficult.

Unless you ultimately want a green card, there is little practical difference between any of these visa categories. Choose the category that facilitates staffing the US business in the quickest and smoothest way possible. Applicants often qualify for several visa categories, and it is important to match the job requirements and applicant's skills with the most appropriate category. The closer the match, the faster the processing.

H-1B VISAS

The H-1B visa is the preferable visa category for professionals. Professional positions include most jobs that require a baccalaureate or higher degree as a minimum requirement. These could include accountant, engineer, economist, teacher, scientist, market researcher, sales engineer, psychiatrist, dietician, forester, hotel manager, librarian, journalist, medical doctor, minister, nutritionist, pharmacist, sociologist, lawyer, veterinarian, vocational counsellor, fashion model, technical publications writer and social worker.

The H-1B visa category can offer simplicity. If the job requires a professional and the applicant has the appropriate professional background, the visa will likely be approved. Although US workers must be notified of the impending H-1B petition. There is no requirement to recruit or hire US workers. There is also no requirement that the applicant have experience in the job offered. Recent college graduates often qualify for H-1B status. On the downside, the notification procedure, Labor Conditions Attestation, though relatively simple, requires additional processing time.

H-1B petitions require:

- information about the applicant's professional abilities

- information about the employer's need for a professional to fill the offered position

- the applicant's resumé

- their educational credentials.

The size of the employer makes little difference in clearly professional positions, such as engineers and accountants. Small companies often have trouble justifying the need for a professional to fill marketing and administrative positions. For example, a small company has little need for the permanent services of a market researcher. The USCIS might suspect that the 'market researcher' who holds an economics or marketing degree is really a salesman.

Small companies generally don't need professionals such as business administration degree holders to fill administrative positions. Most small business managers learn on the job. A baccalaureate degree is usually not a job requirement for the small company business administrator or manager. Large companies with complex management structures fare better in demonstrating the need for business administration, MBA or other business-related degree holders.

Virtually all H-1B applicants have a university degree. Because the law does not require prior work experience, the

USCIS, particularly in the case of young applicants, often questions whether the proposed employment in the US requires the services of a professional. The USCIS may ask for employment advertisements from peer companies that require a university degree for the position, as well as letters from peer companies stating that they believe the position requires a professional education. The USCIS often requests an analysis of the applicant's university study and experience to demonstrate the applicant has the skills to fill the position.

Applicants without a university degree may also qualify for H1-B status. As a rule of thumb three years' work experience equates to one year of university study. Applicants who attended two-year college courses in computer science or related fields and have six years of relevant experience, often successfully qualify for H-1B status. Applicants who failed to finish their liberal arts degree usually make hopeless cases. In any event the USCIS will require a professional credentials evaluator to determine whether the applicant's education and experience equates to a baccalaureate university course of study.

COMMON APPLICATIONS OF H-1 VISAS

Financial and business professionals

Foreign-owned companies often transfer financial and accounting professionals to oversee cost-containment, the purchase of raw materials or parts, preparation of financial reports for the home office, and general accounting and financial activities. Typically the transferee lacks managerial experience and the job in the US rarely contains a managerial component. The lack of managerial experience eliminates any managerial visa possibilities.

As finance-related skills are widely available in the US and usually don't aid US competitiveness, L-1B specialised knowledge or E-1/2 essential skill visas are not recommended for these employees. H-1B status for finance and accounting positions is recommended for four reasons:

- The work falls within established professional disciplines.

- The services of a professional are required to understand financial, accounting or procurement systems.

- The applicant generally has an appropriate university degree (finance, economics or business administration).

- There is no requirement to demonstrate a shortage of US workers or that US workers cannot perform the job.

A typical job description for an economist, accountant or financial officer might be as follows:

'Prepare financial reports, budgets, analyse operating results as compared to budget projections, coordinate home office and subsidiary accounting methods, monitor cost control, prepare and analyse forecasts for executive management, work with outside professionals regarding tax return preparation and financial reporting.'

ENGINEERS

We recommend H-1B visas for non-managerial engineers or scientists (mechanical, electrical and computer engineers, *etc.*) because engineering is a recognised profession usually requiring a related university degree.

Sales engineers often pose difficult cases. Is the sales engineer a salesman or an engineer? Sales managers may qualify for L-1A or E visas; salesmen do not qualify for any visa category. The typical sales engineer holds an engineering-related university degree, works on product development and design, and provides technical support to customers. The sales engineer explains the product in layman's terms.

Companies that manufacture or sell complicated products

in the US hire sales engineers to 'explain the product to the customer, provide technical support to company salesmen, interface with the customer's engineers and technicians, provide customer technical support, and, after warranty service, work with customers' engineers and technicians regarding product modification, and install and monitor maintenance programmes'.

This job description describes sales activity. But the sales engineer also requires technical expertise and a theoretical understanding of the product's mechanics, hence the engineering background. A successful H-1B petition hinges on emphasising the technical aspects of the job. Stress the technical or professional understanding of the product required to make the sale, rather than the salesmanship angle.

Use H-1B when managerial visas are inappropriate and the applicant has a four-year degree relating to a professional discipline. Liberal arts degrees in such areas as literature, business administration, English or other languages are problematic because the degrees only tangentially relate to the job offered.

The H-1B category presents four disadvantages. The duration is limited to six years; it's difficult to go from H-1B to green card status because of the labour certification requirement and the employer must go through the LCA procedure, and there is an up to $1,500 charge in addition to the normal filing fee to fund worker training, scholarships and USCIS operations, plus a $500 fraud fee. Therefore, use the H-1B visa category in the following circumstances:

- The corporate organisation makes the H-1B the only choice.

- If there are choices, use the H-1B if the applicant is young and has little experience and a qualifying BA degree.

SPECIALISED KNOWLEDGE AND ESSENTIAL SKILLS

Companies often transfer specialists who work with a particular product, technology or process. Specialists may qualify for four visa categories: E-1/2 **Essential Skill**, L-1B **Specialized Knowledge**, H-1B **Professional**, or H-2B **Labor Unavailable** in the US.

If the applicant earned a university degree related to his speciality, we recommend H-1B. Such an applicant, for example, would have a Bachelor of Science degree in fisheries for a marine-products specialist, computer science degree for a computer/software specialist, and a forestry degree for a wood products specialist.

It is easier to prove that the university degree relates to the applicant's speciality than to prove that the applicant's skills are essential to the US enterprise (E visa), or an aid to US competitiveness (L-1B). An H-1B visa works because the applicant must use professional skills to understand, modify or analyse a complex product, technology or process.

If a specialist lacks a university degree but holds skills unavailable in the US necessary to the company's success, consider E-1 Essential Skills status. If the specialised skill helps promote US trade or exports, the applicant may qualify for L-1B Specialized Knowledge status. Since both categories face equally intense scrutiny, choose the category that best matches the facts of the case.

L-1B and E-1/2 essential skills refer to the same sorts of skills but with a different emphasis. 'Essential skills' refers to skills critical to the US company's success. In other words, the success of a US business depends upon the applicant's essential skills. Additionally, the essential skills in question must be unavailable in the US. The US treaty company must usually agree to train people to replace the essential skills applicant.

For example, it's often impossible to effectively use foreign machinery without the temporary services of a technician who provides training and technical support. American technicians are unfamiliar with the newly

introduced machinery, so the US treaty company must agree
to train technicians from the US.

Specialised knowledge refers to skills or knowledge of
the parent company's product or processes which must be
transferred to the US subsidiary for increasing the
subsidiary company's competitiveness. The emphasis is on
helping US competitiveness, not the necessity or scarcity of
the skill. Although the US produces many software
engineers, the installation of the parent company's
particular software in the US subsidiary may aid the US
subsidiary's competitiveness in international markets.

Who can use L-1B and E Essential Skills visas?

There's an endless list of appropriate applications for the L-
1B and E essential skills visas. In general, use this category
for persons with technical skills who lack university
degrees. Some points to remember:

- Use another category unless the applicant doesn't
  qualify as an international manager or have a
  professional degree. Professionals and managers may
  also hold specialised knowledge or essential skills.

- The consuls and the USCIS scrutinise L-1 specialised
  knowledge cases and E essential skills cases more than
  managerial or professional cases.

- Use L-1 specialised knowledge when transferring
  knowledge which helps US competitiveness. The
  knowledge does not have to be secret or proprietary. On
  the other hand, if everyone has this knowledge how can
  it aid US competitiveness? A lot of companies make
  instant noodles, but not everyone's instant noodles taste
  the same. The knowledge that makes Company A's
  noodles taste different from its competitor's is
  specialised.

- Use E essential skill status when the emphasis is on
  training US labour to fill a skills shortage. The skill
  must be unavailable in the US and essential to the
  success of the business. Essential does not necessarily

mean complicated. Marine products technicians hold essential skills due to a US skills shortage, not because of the complexity of processing fish.

- The drawback to the E essential skills category is that you may need to agree to train US workers to eliminate the need for an essential skills employee. Because of the training requirements, it's difficult to convince consuls to renew E essential skills visas. Although you can claim high turnover, or changes in technology prevented you from training a replacement, there is a limit to the consul's patience.

- The more esoteric or complicated the skill the easier the case. For example, it's easier to convince consuls or the USCIS that a nuclear physicist working on a new atom-smasher holds more essential skills or specialised knowledge than a noodle technician. In the case of the nuclear physicist, emphasise the complexity of the skill. In the case of the noodle technician, emphasise the contribution to local employment and the export trade.

- Time limits: Consuls issue E visas for up to five years. E visas may be renewed as long as you can convince the consul to issue the visa. There is no limit on extensions. The law limits L-1B visa validity to a total of five continuous years. After the five-year period the applicant must leave the US for a year before applying again.

The 'technicians' option

If the applicant fails to qualify for any other nonimmigrant status, consider the H-2B visa, which applies to skilled or unskilled labour unavailable in the area of intended employment. The key factor here is availability. It does not matter whether you import rocket scientists or ditch diggers as long as the labour is unavailable.

H-2B workers must work seasonally or fill a one-time need. Trainers coming to the US to teach American workers a procedure, such as a chef showing American cooks a new cuisine, fill a one-time need. Theoretically, the trainee takes over the position. This does not apply to child monitors or amahs, who fill a nonrecurring position. The child eventually grows up.

The employer must advertise the position, interview the job applicants, and convince the Department of Labor that none of the job applicants meets the *minimum* job requirements. The Department of Labor establishes minimum job requirements and acceptable salaries, and determines which job applicants to interview. If you succeed with the Department of Labor the job will be certified as available to foreign workers. Then you must petition the USCIS for visa approval.

The entire process takes between 90 and 120 days, and the H-2B visa lasts for one year. To extend the visa the entire process must be repeated.

RECRUITMENT DIFFICULTIES

If there is a choice, use the E-1 essential skills or L-1B specialised knowledge categories because they do not require recruitment. The recruitment process puts the employer in an awkward position. The employer hopes to prove that no qualified US workers exist, and often does that by finding reasons not to hire the people answering the job advertisements. Understandably, the jilted job applicants often complain to the Department of Labor. The cost of advertising and inconvenience of interviewing undesirable applicants often make the process distasteful.

OTHER H-2B APPLICATIONS

Use the H-2B visa when your employees fit into a category of workers who customarily use the H-2B visa, or there is no other choice. Sheep ranchers in Montana use H-2B visas for Basque shepherds. People who want to hire domestic help or someone to take care of their children use H-2B visas for nannies and amahs. Restaurants sometimes use H-2B visas for chefs. Farmers use H-2A (agricultural) for farm workers. Manufacturers, when all else fails, use H-2B for technicians and trainers.

Using the H-2B visa for technical workers–marine products technicians

The marine products industry uses H-2B visas to send technicians to Alaska to process pollack, salmon, herring roe, surimi and other species of fish. The US suffers a shortage of marine products technicians qualified to service foreign markets. Japanese, Korean and Norwegian companies send hundreds of marine products technicians to Alaska on a seasonal basis. The technicians work on short-term contracts. There is a long history of negotiation in this industry, with the USCIS and Department of Labor on one side and the marine products industry in opposition.

The US packer wants to ensure that the product meets buyers' specifications before it reaches the market. The buyer who distributes the products abroad wants assurance that the product meets his market requirements. To meet contractual requirements, the buyer must send its technicians to each packing plant to render technical assistance and quality control. This is a perfect scenario for using H-2B visas.

Since there is no American market for most of the marine products exported to Japan, few qualified US workers exist. And since foreign technicians only work on short-term contracts, there is no sense in applying for long-term visas, such as E-1 essential skills or L-1B specialised knowledge. Employers may spread advertising and recruitment over many visas, as up to 50 technicians often apply at the same time. Advertising and recruitment costs can be prohibitive when applications are made for only a few technicians at a time. Finally, because of its long history of negotiation, the Department of Labor understands the need for foreign technicians and, to an extent, cooperates with the industry.

The marine products industry offers only one example of using the H-2B visa for technical workers. The same approach may be used for all sorts of non-degreed skilled labour, such as welders, machinists, electricians and more.

REVIEW OF GUIDELINES FOR SPECIALISTS

- All things being equal, use L-1B or E essential skills as opposed to H-2B.

- Use E essential skills or L-1B specialised knowledge for long-term technician employees. If an employee only works on a short-term basis, consider the H-2B category.

- Choosing between L-1B or E essential skills visas usually hinges on whether you feel the USCIS or a consul is more receptive to supporting your situation.

- Always apply for the maximum number of H-2B positions. You may have to hire US workers. You want to make sure US workers can be hired while still bringing in your minimum requirement of foreign employees.

- To show good faith in recruiting American workers, provide the Department of Labor with plans to eliminate dependence on foreign workers.

- Remember, cooperate with the Department of Labor during the H-2B process, and don't get frustrated.

BALANCING FOREIGN AND US EMPLOYMENT

The US subsidiary or branch office of a foreign company often employs more alien workers than Americans. Many companies prefer to use their own employees to make large purchases, handle money, or ensure quality control. These factors combine to limit the number of American workers above the secretarial level in the US operation.

Consulates often notice the high ratio of foreign professional workers and strongly suggest hiring more local employees. For immigration purposes, green card holders are US workers. Many companies solve the consular-imposed problem by obtaining green cards for managerial staff.

PREVENTING THE DISCRIMINATION LAWSUIT

Discrimination and sexual harassment law suits most often arise in connection with terminating the employee. The US is a litigious society. Foreign workers, unfortunately, are quick to learn our bad habits.

US workers must be paid the same salary as the foreign worker for the same work. Foreign transferees are often compensated for their overseas work by receiving bonuses paid from abroad as well as enhanced company benefits and housing allowances.

When evaluating the wage discrimination issue, pay close attention to the respective compensation and promotional packages offered to foreign and American workers. If the foreign worker receives a higher compensation package than the US worker for the same work, be prepared to face a lawsuit. Also expect litigation if the US employee does not progress through the company ranks at the same rate as the equally qualified foreign worker. The federal Equal Employment Opportunity Commission often supports such lawsuits in order to uphold anti-discrimination laws.

Branch offices worry less about these types of concerns. Most FCN and BIT treaties, in so many words, give branch offices the right to discriminate in favour of treaty nationals holding E-1 or E-2 visas. There is no right to discriminate in favour of H and L visa holders working for a treaty company. The US Supreme Court made that decision and it's still the law, though it is currently under attack. Given the correct facts, this exception to the civil rights laws may change. This is one of the few advantages of operating as a branch office.

The law requires all employers to provide equal pay for equal work. Equal pay for equal work means general equality of the net result, not identical benefit and compensation packages. Equal pay for equal work, full disclosure of job duties and compensation packages, as well as general fairness, will solve most problems between foreign and local staff members.

Finally, beware of sexual harassment law suits.

Obviously, touching, direct sexual advances and leering constitute sexual harassment. Higher ranking employees imposing themselves on lower ranking employees, as well as off-colour jokes about either sex may constitute sexual harassment. Most insurance companies do not insure corporate officers against sexual harassment law suits. There's only one cure, behave!

9

Five Ways to Obtain a Green Card

Foreign companies move employees to America to staff a business. Foreign nationals, often, establish a US business as a vehicle for permanently moving their families to the US. Among the more common reasons for moving to the US are concerns for safety, fear of instability or unpredictability with the home country's government, children's schooling, quality of life, and retirement.

Investors who merely wish to invest or own property in the US needn't read any more of this chapter. Anyone can buy property, open a bank account, operate a business, or own a house in the US without a visa. Some nations, not the US, permit self-supporting people to retire or reside indefinitely in their country. Although there are proposals in Congress for a retirement visa, for now, people who wish to live, work or retire in the US require a visa.

Moving to a strange country involves planning and patience. Many people require several years to make the transition of living comfortably in the US. People commonly work in the US during the transition period, while the children or family members live in the home country. Everyone who decides to move to America must resolve unique problems. Yet the goal of permanent US residence remains the same. Several visa strategies accomplish this same result:

- Family Class: Application through a close family member.

- Investment in the US.

- Application on the basis of exceptional skills.

- The Two-Step: Managerial transfer.

- Labor Certification: US employer proves that no US workers can fill your job.

UNDERSTANDING GENERAL CONCEPTS

The 'green card' is evidence of Lawful Permanent Residence status. The credit card-sized green card, officially called an Alien Registration Card, although originally green, turned blue, then pink, now pearl white. Despite the changes in colour the green card retained its original name.

Any green card application requires three basic steps:

1. Unless exempted, all employee-based permanent residence applicants must first prove that no American citizens meet the minimum job requirements ('labour certification'). We discuss the following exemptions: exceptional skills, national interest waiver, investment or employment creation, and multinational manager. Family-class green card applicants do not need labour certification.

2. Secondly, the applicant must file an immigrant visa petition with the USCIS on the prescribed form.

3. Currently, if in the US, the final step is the adjustment of status step, and may be filed with the second step, provided the visa number is available. You may also choose to await approval of the second step then consular process, which would be substantially faster processing.

Petitioning for permanent residence status

The green card petition requests classification as a particular category of permanent residence. Family class applicants use Form I-130, employment class applicants use Form I-140, and investors use Form I-526. The petition and supporting documents are filed at an USCIS Regional Processing Center. The applicant then must wait for the result. The USCIS will either issue an approval letter, deny the application, or ask for more information. The USCIS has announced that no I–130s will be processed until the priority date is near. This could be ten years or more, depending upon the category. For example, a first preference application (unmarried, over 21 years of age, son or daughter of a US citizen) may carry only a two–three year quota wait, while a fourth preference (sibling of a US citizen) can take close to twenty years, depending upon the nationality. Upon petition approval, assuming a visa is available, applicants may proceed to the next step, the interview.

Green card petitions include spouses and children under age 21, as of the approval date of the adjustment of status or consular application. For example, your child turned 21 on 1 March 1999 and you filed the adjustment of status documents on 1 December 1999. If the USCIS approves the adjustment of status to permanent residence on 2 March 1999, the 21-year-old child may not qualify.

The Child Status Protection Act 2002 subtracts the time that the USCIS spent adjudicating the permanent residence petition, which could be considerable, from the child's age. If the visa became available when the child turned 21 years and 4 months and the USCIS took five months to adjudicate the permanent residence petition, the five months is subtracted from the child's age reducing the child's age to something less than age 21 and the child qualifies. This new law solves many, but not all of the problems associated with children turning 21 before the visa becomes available.

Waiting for visa availability

In order to obtain permanent residence status, the USCIS must approve the preference petition and a visa must be available. Petitioners often encounter a waiting period. This 'quota wait' occurs between the petition filing date and the date a visa becomes available.

The US quota system seeks to limit annual permanent residence visas to approximately 480,000 family class, 140,000 employment class, 10,000 special immigrants (such as investors), and 55,000 diversity class (called lottery) divided among the various permanent residence categories. The quota exempts immediate relatives, spouses, parents and children of US citizens who may interview immediately after visa approval.

The visa allocation formula annually grants each country or group of countries approximately 25,000 visas. Quota waits occur when a country uses its annual visa allotments plus unused visas from other countries. For example, high demand from countries such as Korea, China, India and Mexico has caused a minimum nine-year quota wait for brothers and sisters of US citizens of these origins. On the other hand, most employment-based categories experience no quota wait.

The waiting period begins on the date (called the 'priority date') of filing the petition with the USCIS or Department of Labor, as the case may be. Persons holding a current priority date may file for the interview. The State Department publishes *The Visa Bulletin*, which lists current priority dates by category once a month. Because visa demand varies by country and visa category, there is no way to accurately predict the movement of priority dates.

Going on the dole

Green card holders are ineligible for social security, national pension benefits, and Medicare benefits unless they have worked one day in each of 40 calendar quarters or ten years. Green card holders may qualify for social security disability benefits. The calendar quarters do not have to be consecutive. State governments may at their discretion offer green card holders some welfare benefits. Missing social security may not be too big a deal; it may not be around by the time many of us need it.

Guaranteeing you won't go on the dole

All family class green card applicants must be guaranteed by a US citizen or permanent resident. The guarantor must guarantee that the applicant will not be a public charge for ten years. See Form I-864. Employment-based applicants have little problem because they have a job and an employer. Individuals often have problems with the guarantor requirements.

The guarantor, a US citizen or green card holder living in the USA, must prove an annual income of at least 125 per cent of the poverty minimum. The actual amount depends upon family size. The charts are updated annually. Those without a guarantor, often lottery winners and spouses of green card holders or US citizens living abroad, are simply out of luck unless they can find an immigrant's aid organisation or surety who is willing to serve as a guarantor.

Getting sick without insurance

The US does not have a national health system for persons under 62 years of age. Medicare is a national health system for those over 62 years of age. The US government determines the doctors' rates and acts as a single payor. All doctors must participate in the programme. There is no supplementary insurance and doctors may not charge more than the Medicare rates, even to willing customers.

As in the case of social security benefits, green card holders are ineligible for Medicare unless they work for 40 calendar quarters. Most green card holders must either pay for private health coverage or be prepared to fly home in case of serious illness.

BEING INTERVIEWED FOR PERMANENT RESIDENCE STATUS

The interview verifies eligibility for an immigration classifica-tion, and checks for grounds of exclusion from the US. Grounds for exclusion include criminal records, undesirable political affiliations, certain diseases, and lack of financial support. You may have your interview with the USCIS at an office nearest your US residence, or you may attend an interview with the US Consulate nearest your place of foreign residence. The USCIS process is called an **Adjustment of Status to Permanent Residence**. The consular process is called **Application for Immigrant Visa and Alien Registration**. Both processes achieve the same ultimate results.

The term 'Adjust Status to Permanent Residence' refers to the procedures required to change from a nonimmigrant status to a permanent resident. No aliens except for immediate relatives may be interviewed in the US without being of legal status. Aliens in illegal status must be interviewed at a Consulate abroad.

The USCIS and consulates require the same basic information and tend to ask the same interview questions. In choosing whether to be interviewed with the USCIS or a Consulate, consider local processing times, local enforcement policies and convenience, which vary among USCIS offices and consular posts.

CHOOSING BETWEEN ADJUSTMENT OF STATUS AND CONSULAR PROCESSING

Consular processing can be faster, four to six months compared with two–three years, with the forecast of much longer in the near future. One may not travel during the adjustment of status processing period without applying for special travel permission, **advance parole**. If one travels without advance parole, the USCIS may deem the adjustment of status petition abandoned. The applicant may be denied admission to the US or have to refile and start the adjustment of status proceedings from the beginning.

Advance parole requires a separate petition and filing fee, takes 30–60 days to process, and is usually valid for 1 year. Although the advance parole provides for multiple entries to the US during its validity period, the adjustment of status proceedings often take several years. If you intend to travel frequently it's often more convenient to have the interview with a Consulate abroad.

People fearing strict consular enforcement often choose to have their interview with the USCIS. If problems arise they may remain in the US while solving the problem. If problems occur during a consular interview, you must usually remain abroad until they are resolved. Also, appeals of an USCIS decision can be made to an independent court. If a consul denies an application the matter must be resolved with the US State Department. No independent judges review consular decisions.

WORKING DURING THE ADJUSTMENT OF STATUS PROCESSING

Adjustment of status applicants may simultaneously apply for employment authorisation. The applicant should receive a laminated card authorising employment within 90 days of applying.

Many employment-based green card applicants want to change jobs or be self-employed as soon as they get their green card. Although the employment authorisation card permits you to work for any employer, the petitioning employer and employee must intend a permanent, or at least long-term, employment relationship. If the USCIS were to discover that the employee had no intention of working for the petitioning employer, it could revoke the green card. Employees must work for the petitioning employer until the preference application is approved, and the adjustment has been pending at least 180 days before becoming portable, that is, able to change employers. Any change of employers must be in the same field of work as the application.

GREEN CARD CATEGORIES

Let's examine the various approaches to obtaining a green card, and explore the easiest options first.

Pursuing the easiest method first – family class
Family class petitions require proof of a qualifying relationship. Qualifying relationships include:

- *Immediate relative*: Parents, spouses of US citizens, unmarried children under 21 years of age.

- *1st preference*: Unmarried children of US citizens.

- *2nd preference*: Spouses and unmarried children of permanent residents (unmarried children under 21 [2A] have priority over unmarried children over 21 [2B]).

- *3rd preference*: Married children of US citizens.

- *4th preference*: Brothers and sisters of adult US citizens.

'Family class' merely requires proof of the qualifying family relationship. Most people do not use lawyers for family class cases, except for convenience or in the case of missing or nonexistent records. In most cases, if you can't prove that your mother is your mother, there is a problem no lawyer can solve. You may want to consult with an expert to guide you through the filing and interview procedures, help you organise important evidence and assist with timing.

Petitioning for family class status
The petition (Form I-130) generally requires proof of the status of the sponsoring relative and proof of relationship with the benificiary relative. To prove the required family relationship, attach the applicant's and sponsor's birth certificates, and provide proof of the sponsor's US citizenship or permanent resident status. The instructions on the I-130 Form suggest appropriate supporting documents and explain the filing procedures.

PLANNING FOR THE QUOTA WAITING PERIOD

The quota waiting period – the period beginning after visa approval and ending with visa availability – presents the biggest obstacle in family class cases, since it may cause several years of separation from family members. Adult siblings of US citizens usually work or manage businesses during the waiting period. Spouses and parents of American citizens experience no quota wait. The most common problem concerns spouses and children of green card holders.

A typical scenario: A husband with a green card marries a foreigner. The husband files for a green card and the USCIS approves a second preference petition for the new wife. A two-year quota wait is projected. The wife has no visa status other than a tourist visa.

What does this couple do during the quota waiting period? If the wife wants to live in the US with her husband, rather than merely visiting him, she will need independent visa status. Two choices should be examined here. The wife may find a job that leads to an independent visa, such as H-1B or E, or attend school on an F-1 visa. If neither of these visas can be arranged, the wife can only have short-term visits with her husband.

Depending on nationality, one may visit the US on visa waiver or with a B-2 tourist visa. Since visa waiver limits the visit to 90 days with no extensions, most spouses prefer a B-2 visa. As a rule, consuls do not issue B-2 visas to foreign spouses coming to the US to visit their American mates. If possible, apply for the B-2 visa before marrying.

Negotiating the waiting period with a B-2 visa

Most B-2 visas allow multiple entries over a five-year period. The USCIS usually admits B-2 visa holders for six months, and it's relatively easy to extend for an additional six months. But subsequent extensions are difficult. Plan on returning home after the one-year period. The second preference waiting period for spouses of green card holders is approximately two years. The B-2 visa method usually covers one of the two years.

Aliens cannot come to the US on a temporary visa when they intend to live permanently in the country. The USCIS generally assumes that a wife coming to visit her husband or vice versa intends to live with the spouse. The chances of entering the US may depend upon convincing an USCIS inspector that the visit is truly temporary.

It is easier to demonstrate intentions for *temporary* visits to the US if you have a job, family and property in your home country. For obvious reasons, the longer you stay home between trips the more clear it is that there are meaningful ties to your home country. Factors which prove an intention to return home after a short visit include a job or business in the home country, a residence, family, and proof that you've returned home after previous US visits.

Be honest, prepare supporting evidence, and make sure the USCIS appreciates the applicant's knowledge and understanding of the rules. Under the Summary Removal rules an USCIS officer may deny entry and prohibit future entries for five years if the officer believes that the applicant for entry misrepresented material facts. There's no hearing, no appeal, and no recourse other than to file a waiver of the grounds of exclusion with a consulate abroad. Waiver processing takes several months and, worse than that, requires consent of the Consul and the USCIS, thus reducing the chances of approval. The moral of the story is, whatever you do, don't lie!

The V visa.

The new V visa permits persons with an approved I-130 preference petition to join their US green card spouse if they have been waiting three or more years from the approval date of the I-130 preference petition. The V visa permits the applicant to work in the US and remain in the US with rights to travel until the quota becomes available. This means the maximum period of separation for those who marry a US permanent resident is three years plus the I-130 and V visa processing time.

Negotiating the quota waiting period by finding a job

Holders of university degrees may seek a sponsoring

employer and explore the filing of an H-1B petition. If the spouse finds an employer of the same nationality qualified for E visa status, consider an E visa. Visa waiver or B-2 visa holders may legally look for jobs in the US. B-2 visa holders may find a job and change status in the US.

Many people change from B-2 to H-1B or E visa status and wait in the US, without leaving, until the green card is available. Since visa waiver holders may not change to another nonimmigrant status in the US after finding employment, they must obtain USCIS approval and return home to apply for the visa. All nonimmigrant visa applicants must disclose the green card applications submitted on their behalf. The USCIS cannot deny nonimmigrant work visa petitions solely because of a pending green card application.

Negotiating the quota waiting period as a student

Some spouses go to school as F-1 students. This option works for those who intend to go to school or want to continue school but need a compelling reason to do so. Only serious students need apply, as a full course load must be maintained in order to keep the F-1 visa.

Summary

If the quota waiting period separates a foreign family member from a US relative, there are four choices:

- waiting at home

- visiting the US

- finding an American job and changing to a nonimmigrant work visa

- or going to school and changing to F-1 status.

In all cases you must be able to prove your intention to return home at the end of the temporary stay, in spite of a pending green card petition.

INVESTING IN AMERICA FOR A GREEN CARD

The US, like Canada, Australia, New Zealand and other countries, has an immigrant investor programme. The US requires an investment of $1,000,000 in a trade or business, and employment of ten full-time persons. The American programme is officially called the Employment Creation Aliens Program, or more commonly, the Investor Visa. The programme reduces the investment amount to $500,000 for rural or high-unemployment areas.

The US programme began in 1990. One of our first immigrant investor cases involved a mother and her two daughters, each of whom purchased 16.66 per cent of a construction company and large shopping mall. The husband had given the mother and each daughter $1,000,000, a total of $3,000,000, in a divorce settlement. The funds came from a US bank account. Although the mother and daughters served on the company's board of directors, they had no active roles in daily management. The project employed about 45 people, some on a part-time basis. This case satisfied the regulatory requirements and was duly approved.

The EB-5 visa category started in 1991. Regional Centres started in 1993. The USCIS suspended the EB-5 program in 1997. Several companies competed for investment capital during this period. Most of the companies didn't offer sound investments and were really in business to collect fees rather than to fund an ongoing business. Many investment opportunities didn't raise the full $500,000 or $1,000,000 investment capital or hire the required number of employees.

The USCIS, rightly wanted to stop these abuses of the programme. In 1998, the USCIS wrongly applied their revised rules retroactively to people who already had approved petitions. The USCIS attempted to revoke these visa petitions. This started the litigation. In 2002, Congress passed a new law to protect the pre-1998 investors. Also, in 2002, in a case commonly known as 'Chang' the 9th Circuit Court of Appeals ruled that the USCIS may not apply their new rules retroactively.

In August of 2003, the USCIS began approving regional centre petitions for the first time since 1998. EB-5 petitions based on sound investments, with the full investment amount, with proper supporting documentation, should continue to be approved.

Employee criteria

Any trade or business that employs at least ten persons per investor qualifies for this programme. You may start a business, buy a business, or invest in an existing commercial concern. The investment must increase the capital or employment of an existing business by at least 140 per cent. The people in the example above invested in an existing business.

Immigrant investors may hold minority interests in the business. Although investors must play a role in management, the regulations deem limited partners or members of the board of directors as active participants in management. As long as the business employs at least ten persons per investor, it may accept as many investors who make the required investment.

A 'full-time employee' is defined as someone working at least 37.5 hours per week, but employers may combine part-time employees to satisfy the definition. Twenty people who work 18.75 hours each equals ten employees. Independent contractors, such as trades people and cleaning service personnel, do not count as employees. Employees may not be immediate family members of the investor, but must be US citizens or green card holders.

PAYING BY CASH OR CREDIT

The law permits instalment payments of the required investment amount. Many investment programmes offer instalment payment plans or provide unsecured financing. The USCIS does its best to deny petitions where the investment amount is paid in anything but one lump sum at the time of green card approval. Loans must be secured by the investor's assets. The investment amount may be placed in an escrow or trust account, provided the trust agreement states that the funds will be released to the business or target investment upon green card approval.

Investment fund sources

Investment funds may come from any legal foreign or US source, including gifts and divorce settlements. Applicants must be prepared to show the source of their investment funds. Corporate investors may not designate an employee or shareholder to receive the green card. Whoever receives the visa must make the investment. Borrowed investment funds qualify as long as the borrowed funds are secured by the assets of applicant but not the target US business. For example, investors may borrow against a home and use the loan proceeds to buy a business qualifying for the investor visa.

Business plan

The USCIS application, Form I-526, must include a business plan which details the application of funds to the target investment and demonstrates that the target business will support at least ten employees. The business plan should contain the level of detail one would provide a bank with to secure a commercial loan.

Investors have two years to make the investment and hire ten employees. The USCIS grants a conditional green card upon the initial investment, and two years later issues an unrestricted green card upon verification of the required employees and capital. There is no requirement to continue the investment beyond the two-year period.

Applicant suitability

Unlike Canada, Australia and New Zealand the US does not have investor suitability standards or a points system. There are no language or business experience requirements. The US investor must only prove the legal source of his investment capital.

Proving a legal source of funds may not be so simple. The USCIS often denies petitions where the investor's tax returns do not show sufficient gross income over a five-year period to demonstrate how someone could accumulate the required investment amount. In such cases, proof of sales of assets, inheritance, loans or gifts may suffice.

THE REGIONAL CENTRE PROGRAMME

The ten employee requirement deters most investors. To encourage immigrant investors, the USCIS, in 1994, devised a slightly different scheme. Now immigrant investors may invest in USCIS-approved funds called **regional centres**. The regional centres are any project, private or public, that promotes US employment and exports in a particular region of the US.

The regional centre programme permits those who have money, but do not want to manage a US business and hire US workers, to obtain green cards. In this programme the promoter makes a proposal to the USCIS in Washington, D.C. to develop a region or area. If the USCIS believes the proposal will benefit a regional economy and shows potential for providing significant employment opportunities, the project will be designated a regional centre. With USCIS approval in hand, the promoter forms a limited partnership or corporation to raise money for specific projects.

Foreign investors may apply for green cards upon depositing their investment capital into an independent bank trust or escrow account. The investor's funds must be released to the closing agent for the designated project immediately upon visa approval.

Investors in a regional centre do not have to prove the business will employ ten persons. Instead, the regional centre may rely on government for its particular projects. For example, a regional centre proposing to develop an air cargo facility may rely on the indirect employment created by the air cargo facility to satisfy the ten-employee requirement. Indirect employment includes direct employment plus jobs such as service industries that rely on the regional centre. If the job multiplier statistics demonstrate the regional centre will create 500 direct and indirect jobs, the regional centre may seek 50 investors. Most state economic development agencies provide job multiplier statistics.

Except for employment creation, regional centres must follow the same rules as those for the immigrant investor programme in the employment creation criteria.

Who manages regional centres?

Individuals, corporations and government agencies are eligible to manage regional centre projects. Local governments were responsible for sponsoring two of the first seven funds. Our law firm has established several privately-managed funds. Since government can also mismanage money, don't be comforted by its sponsorship of a fund.

For obvious reasons, very few people used the immigrant investor programme at the $1,000,000 level. Regional centres located in rural or high-unemployment areas, *ie* the $500,000 investments, are becoming popular. Agents representing several Immigrant Investment companies around the world offer a variety of regional centre investment opportunities. We carefully monitor regional centre activity, but because of rapid changes we did not publish activity lists in this book.

Some pitfalls with the immigrant investor category

Investment immigration is controversial. Although the emphasis is on investment, some people see nothing more than the privileged rich buying into their country. The immigration departments of Canada, US, New Zealand and Australia have at one time or another suspended their programmes, delayed processing petitions, or changed rules without notice. Successful investors put up with the uncertainty. Patience generally prevails.

If the investment fails within the two-year conditional green card period, investors could lose their money and green cards. The USCIS has no plan to deal with this unfortunate possibility.

Who should apply under the immigrant investor programme

If you want to own and operate a business that requires at least $500,000 capital and ten employees, the immigrant investor programme is for you. Otherwise, first investigate whether you qualify for a visa category that doesn't require at least $500,000 capital. If not, then consider the regional centre programme because it does not have the ten employee requirement.

The regional centre programme has been most often used by:

- Retirees who want to reside permanently in the US without working. You may not live in the US, whether or not you work, without a permanent residence visa. Typically, visits to the vacation home increase in duration to the point where the immigration inspector determines you live in the US and need a green card. At that point you have a home that you can't use without a green card.

- Parents who want green cards for their children so that they can attend US public schools without paying tuition, or attend lower-cost state universities (foreign students may only attend US public high schools for 12 months without paying tuition).

- Young people of means who want to start life in America.

- Non-citizens who wish to bring their parents to the US permanently.

- People of both sexes who, rather than risk embarrassing families, buy green cards for their lovers, who are happy living in the US while the sponsor enjoys reduced risks.

SUMMARISING THE IMMIGRANT INVESTMENT CATEGORY

The immigrant investment category provides the fastest, most expensive and safest way to get a green card. Investors may be assured of getting the visa before their funds are committed to the investment because capital may remain in a trust account until visa approval. E and L visa applicants must commit funds to the investment before filing their visa petition.

The biggest disadvantage to the immigrant investor programme, aside from the costs, is that immigrant investors receive a two-year conditional green card. The USCIS verifies the bona fides of the regional centre investment at the end of the two-year period. What happens if USCIS changes the rules mid-stream? What happens if the investment fails? The United States Court of Appeals for the 9th District answered the first question. In 2003 the Court ruled in the case of 'Chang' that the USCIS may not change its rules and apply them retroactively to people that already invested. In the second instance nobody knows because it hasn't happened yet.

RETIRING IN AMERICA: 'THE TWO-STEP' METHOD FOR MANAGERS, EXECUTIVES AND ENTREPRENEURS

As the fastest and easiest method for business people to obtain green cards, the **Two-Step Method** permits international managers and executives to apply for green cards without labour certification. The exemption from labour certification saves considerable time and expense. 'The two-step' works for managerial/executive transferees working for established international organisations, as well as for the small business people who create an international organisation and transfer themselves to manage the US operation.

Step 1 refers to transferring in a managerial capacity to the US within an international organisation. This requires establishing a US business qualifying as an L-1 international organisation, or using an existing L-1 international organisation and obtaining a nonimmigrant work visa as a managerial transfer.

The applicant must have worked in a managerial or executive capacity on the foreign side of the international organisation for one of the three years prior to the transfer to the US branch, subsidiary or affiliate of the foreign employer in a managerial or executive capacity.

Step 2 refers to the green card procedures, which may occur at any time after the US employer has been doing business for one year.

The two-step applies to international managers and executives regardless of visa type. Therefore, managers and executives may use H-1B, E-1/2 pr H-1B visas. The exemption from labour certification focuses on transfer in a managerial capacity within an international organisation, not the particular visa used to effect the transfer.

A common scenario

Let's look at how the two-step might work for an individual. A 'Mr Smith' owns an electric motor parts trading company in a foreign country. He wants his children to receive an American education, and his wife wants to live in the US with the children while they attend school. The Smiths ultimately want to retire in the US, so Mr Smith needs a long-term visa strategy for the entire family.

The first step

Mr Smith establishes a US subsidiary company and secures an office. He then applies for an L-1A visa to manage the new American company during the start-up phase. Smith's wife and children receive L-2 visas as dependants, thus allowing them to attend school. Mrs Smith is allowed to work unless she files, separately, for work authorisation. The L-1A must be extended after the first year. Managers of start-up companies must establish the company within one year. Mr Smith applies for and receives a three-year extension. Mrs Smith and the children must also file for extension of their status, and if desired, Mrs/ Smith must file for extension of her work authorisation.

The second step
Immediately after the extension approval, Mr Smith applies for approval as an 'International Manager or Executive'. Upon approval, he submits documents for the family. If all goes well Mr Smith will receive a temporary green card within two to four years of his petition, and he should receive a permanent green card about four months later. Within five years after arriving in America, Mr Smith, his wife and their children under 21 years of age will have green cards.

If Mr Smith transfers to a company established in the US for at least one year he may immediately apply for a green card. The exemption from labour certification depends upon managerial/executive transfer within an international organisation that has been doing business in the US for at least one year. The applicant needn't work in the US for one year. Theoretically, the applicant could apply from abroad as long as the international organisation conducted business in the US for one year, as the one-year period refers to the employer, not the applicant.

DETAILS OF THE TWO-STEP PROCESS

Step 1: Establish the US business/managerial transfer with a nonimmigrant work visa

Establishing a US subsidiary
Establishing a company means:

- incorporating a business

- obtaining federal tax identification numbers

- finding a place of business

- getting relevant licences.

For a variety of tax and legal reasons, we recommend establishing a US corporation rather than a US branch office. In most cases, the applicant should issue shares to the foreign employer, which becomes the parent company. The subsidiary company must either lease or buy a place of doing business. Do not operate from a personal residence because the USCIS will query it.

The US company may buy property, purchase a business, or start a new firm, and conduct any business as long as it requires the services of a manager or executive. As a general rule, the business must hire employees; a one-person operation does not require a manager. The business plan should require at least three or four employees.

Any business qualifies for the two-step: real estate investment, import/export trader, merchant, manufacturer, restaurant manager or manager of a group of professionals. In fact, the US trade or business may be unrelated to the foreign parent's line of business. The foreign parent could be a trading company, while the US subsidiary could be a real estate management firm.

Choosing a nonimmigrant work visa
For green card purposes, any nonimmigrant work visa suffices as long as you transfer to the US branch, subsidiary or affiliate of the foreign employer in a managerial capacity. Established companies generally use the L-1A or E-1/2 options. Although H-1B visa holders may also serve in a managerial capacity, we don't recommend using H-1B status as a stepping stone in the two-step process. Consider the time and effort required to convince the USCIS that the H-1B professional also serves in a managerial position. The USCIS would want a convincing explanation as to why a managerial visa was not used in the first place. Most start-up companies should use the L-1A visa. Examine all visa options. Just make sure to transfer to the US as a manager.

Factors such as the nature of the US business, nationality, convenience, and consular *vs* USCIS enforcement policies, determine whether application

U.S. Customs and Border Protection

Customs Declaration

19 CFR 122.27, 148.12, 148.13, 148.110, 148.111, 1498; 31 CFR 5316

FORM APPROVED
OMB NO. 1651-0009

Each arriving traveler or responsible family member must provide the following information (only ONE written declaration per family is required):

1. Family **Name**

   First *(Given)*   Middle

2. **Birth date**   Day   Month   Year

3. Number of **Family members** traveling with you

4. (a) U.S. Street **Address** (hotel name/destination)

   (b) City   (c) State

5. **Passport issued by** (country)

6. **Passport number**

7. Country of **Residence**

8. **Countries visited** on this trip prior to U.S. arrival

9. **Airline/Flight No.** or **Vessel Name**

10. The primary purpose of this trip is **business**:   Yes   No

11. I am (We are) bringing

    (a) fruits, vegetables, plants, seeds, food, insects: Yes   No

    (b) meats, animals, animal/wildlife products: Yes   No

    (c) disease agents, cell cultures, snails: Yes   No

    (d) soil or have been on a farm/ranch/pasture: Yes   No

12. I have (We have) been in close proximity of (such as touching or handling) **livestock**:   Yes   No

13. I am (We are) carrying **currency or monetary instruments** over $10,000 U.S. or foreign equivalent: (see definition of monetary instruments on reverse)   Yes   No

14. I have (We have) **commercial merchandise**: (articles for sale, samples used for soliciting orders, or goods that are not considered personal effects)   Yes   No

15. **Residents** — the **total value of all goods**, including commercial merchandise I/we have purchased or acquired abroad, (including gifts for someone else, but not items mailed to the U.S.) and am/are bringing to the U.S. is: $

    Visitors — the **total value of all articles** that will remain in the U.S., including commercial merchandise is: $

Read the instructions on the back of this form. Space is provided to list all the items you must declare.

I HAVE READ THE IMPORTANT INFORMATION ON THE REVERSE SIDE OF THIS FORM AND HAVE MADE A TRUTHFUL DECLARATION.

X _____

(Signature)   Date (day/month/year)

For Official Use Only

CBP Form 6059B (01/04)

U.S. Customs and Border Protection
Welcomes You to the United States

U.S. Customs and Border Protection is responsible for protecting the United States against the illegal importation of prohibited items. CBP officers have the authority to question you and to examine you and your personal property. If you are one of the travelers selected for an examination, you will be treated in a courteous, professional, and dignified manner. CBP Supervisors and Passenger Service Representatives are available to answer your questions. Comment cards are available to compliment or provide feedback.

Important Information

U.S. Residents — declare all articles that you have acquired abroad and are bringing into the United States.

Visitors (Non-Residents) — declare the value of all articles that will remain in the United States.

Declare all articles on this declaration form and show the value in U.S. dollars. For gifts, please indicate the retail value.

Duty — CBP officers will determine duty. U.S. residents are normally entitled to a duty-free exemption of $800 on items accompanying them. Visitors (non-residents) are normally entitled to an exemption of $100. Duty will be assessed at the current rate on the first $1,000 above the exemption.

Controlled substances, obscene articles, and toxic substances are generally prohibited entry. Agriculture products are restricted entry.

Thank You, and Welcome to the United States.

The transportation of currency or **monetary instruments,** regardless of the amount, is legal. However, if you bring in to or take out of the United States more than $10,000 (U.S. or foreign equivalent, or a combination of both), you are required by law to file a report on FinCEN 105 (formerly Customs Form 4790) with U.S. Customs and Border Protection. Monetary instruments include coin, currency, travelers checks and bearer instruments such as personal or cashiers checks and stocks and bonds. If you have someone else carry the currency or monetary instrument for you, you must also file a report on FinCEN 105. Failure to file the required report or failure to report the *total* amount that you are carrying may lead to the seizure of *all* the currency or monetary instruments, and may subject you to civil penalties and/or criminal prosecution. SIGN ON THE OPPOSITE SIDE OF THIS FORM AFTER YOU HAVE READ THE IMPORTANT INFORMATION ABOVE AND MADE A TRUTHFUL DECLARATION.

Description of Articles (List may continue on another CBP Form 6059B)	Value	CBP Use Only
Total		

PAPERWORK REDUCTION ACT NOTICE: The Paperwork Reduction Act says we must tell you why we are collecting this information, how we will use it, and whether you have to give it to us. The information collected on this form is needed to carry out the Customs, Agriculture, and currency laws of the United States. CBP requires the information on this form to insure that travelers are complying with these laws and to allow us to figure and collect the right amount of duty and tax. Your response is mandatory. An agency may not conduct or sponsor, and a person is not required to respond to a collection of information, unless it displays a valid OMB control number. The estimated average burden associated with this collection of information is 4 minutes per respondent or record keeper depending on individual circumstances. Comments concerning the accuracy of this burden estimate and suggestions for reducing this burden should be directed to U.S. Customs and Border Protection, Reports Clearance Officer, Information Services Branch, Washington, DC 20229, and to the Office of Management and Budget, Paperwork Reduction Project (1651-0009), Washington, DC 20503. **THIS FORM MAY NOT BE REPRODUCED WITHOUT APPROVAL FROM THE CBP FORMS MANAGER.**

CBP Form 6059B (01/04)

should be made for E-1, E-2 or L-1A status. The USCIS will grant an initial one-year validity period for L-1A start-up companies. At the end of the one-year period the USCIS requires proof of progress toward establishing the US business. Consuls often deny E visa status for start-up companies.

E or L managers may be paid from the foreign parent company and commute between the US office and overseas locations. two-step managers may work part-time in the US. However, two-step managers must prove they exercise managerial control over the US business. Proof of managerial control includes authority to sign company documents, a history of reviewing company operations, management memoranda, minutes of management decisions, contract negotiation, hiring and firing, and budgetary authority.

Step 2: One year of doing business, multinational manager green card

Apply for the green card as a first preference multinational manager any time after the US company has been doing business in the US for one year.

'Doing business' means:

- regularly and systematically providing goods and services to customers.

The USCIS verifies gross sales, employment and business activity. Remember that most managers must hire subordinate employees to prove service in a managerial capacity. Persons managing a function or a division of a large company, *ie* a regional sales manager, do not need subordinate employees. This exception to the employee requirement does not help many small business applicants.

The 'one year of doing business' requirement means that the company did business in the US for a year. It does not mean that the individual, the transferee, worked in the US for a year. In other words, the applicant's foreign company can buy an established US business with a multi-year operating history. Since the US business operated for over one year, it means immediate transfer of the person to the new US subsidiary as a first preference multinational manager, skipping the first step of the two-step.

Beware of the many unscrupulous operators, principally in Pakistan, India, Taiwan, Korea, and China, who offer ready-made businesses for sale to those wishing to eliminate the first step of the two-step. Before joining such a scheme consider the Consul's surprise when he sees that a substantial manufacturing company needs a manager for its newly purchased dry cleaning franchise in New York.

ANOTHER TWO-STEP APPROACH

Green cards for corporate executives or managers and established organisations

Corporate executives and managers for established international organisations use the same two-step process as individual businessmen, but they benefit from a ready-made international organisation. Individual business people must create their own international organisation.

As a rule, an employer transfers a manager to a US member of the international organisation using an L-1 or E-1/2 visa. In the typical situation the manager worked in a managerial capacity for a member of the international organisation for one of the three years prior to being transferred to the US. The American operation has been doing business for more than one year prior to the transfer. This type of manager may apply for a green card immediately upon arrival in the US. Theoretically, the manager could apply for a green card before transfer while working for the parent company abroad.

Benefits for children and retirement
Many people seek green cards because their children want to attend an American university or they plan to retire in the US. Dependent children need a separate visa to remain in the US after the age of 21, usually F-1 student or a nonimmigrant work visa. At retirement, an executive or

manager will no longer be an employee of an international organisation. Upon retirement he must apply for a green card through investment, skills or family ties types of petitions. It's easier to obtain a green card as a multinational manager because of the exemption from labour certification.

Children under age 21 may simultaneously obtain green cards through parents as well as find a job after graduation without having to apply for a work visa. As a permanent US resident, the child may qualify for lower-cost resident tuition at state universities (private universities usually charge the same expensive tuition to all students). The savings in state university tuition for one child more than pay for any immigration legal fees, and is one of the better investments you can make.

Employer's point of view
Many employers resist employees' green card applications since green card holders may work anywhere they choose. After all, why go through the time and expense of a green card application only to lose an employee after they receive the green card? Conversely, nonimmigrant visa holders may only work for the sponsoring employer.

The law requires the employer to intend to hire the applicant permanently and the applicant to intend to work permanently for the petitioning employer. Thanks to President Lincoln, employers cannot force employees to work for them and it is virtually impossible to prove preconceived intent to leave the employer upon green card approval. Thus petitioning employers always risk losing their prize recruit to the competition the minute the green card is in hand.

While there is no perfect solution to this problem, many employers withhold the legal fees from the employee's salary for a period of several years to at least ensure they don't lose the legal fees and the employee. Some employers simply make the applicant pay for the green card legal fees. The latter approach almost ensures the loss of the employee because the employee feels he paid for his freedom.

Most middle-aged green card applicants worked their entire careers for a single corporate group, and it is difficult to find an equivalent job in the US. The middle-aged applicant usually won't move to a new company in a foreign land at the middle or end of their careers. Most want to spend more time on the golf course or in other leisure activities rather than undergo a mid-life career change. Those new to the corporate group pose a greater risk of using the employer to obtain a green card and then leaving.

Foreign-owned US employers may benefit when an executive or manager obtains a green card. Employers must file an Embassy Annual Report for E visa purposes, listing US and foreign workers and their positions. The embassy uses this report to monitor how many E visas it will grant for particular positions. Green card holders count as American workers and may free up a new E visa position.

TIMING AND PROCEDURE

Nonimmigrant work visa (Step 1)

File L-1A petitions at an USCIS regional centre. File E visa petitions at a consul or regional processing centre if in the US. USCIS filings require Form 129 and an L or E Supplement. Each consulate uses its own forms. Expect L-1A or E-1/2 visa processing to take between 30 and 60 days.

E visa processing times depend on a particular consulate's policies. Unless buying or working for an existing business, you must wait until the US business can prove one year of active operation before applying for the green card. In two-step cases the green card application contains much of the same information as the L-1A or E visa petition.

Green card (Step 2)

File Form I-140 (Petition for Immigrant Worker) and supporting documents with the USCIS at a regional service centre. Allow up to six months for petition processing. Upon petition approval, file for a green card interview with the USCIS or consulate. Currently, multinational managers endure no quota waiting period.

ATTENDING THE GREEN CARD INTERVIEW

USCIS interview

Most two-step applicants have their interview with the USCIS because their families already live in the US. Choose whether to be interviewed with the USCIS or a consulate on the I-140 petition. To interview in the US, file the Adjustment of Status Package (Form I-485) and supporting documents with the USCIS. Most USCIS offices only conduct personal interviews for suspect business-class cases. Otherwise, the USCIS merely reviews the adjustment of status documents, verifies police records, and usually mails the result and, hopefully, a temporary green card about a year after the filing. The temporary green card should be followed by the permanent green card within four months. Adjustment procedures vary among the USCIS district offices.

Consular interview

Alternatively, you may have your interview at a consulate. In the case of consular interviews, the USCIS sends files to a visa distribution centre in New Hampshire, called the National Visa Center (NVC). The NVC sends a biographical information package (called 'Packet 3') to the applicant and forwards the file to the correct consular post. The consulate contacts the applicant with interview details. Interview procedures vary among consular offices. Applicants generally receive a temporary green card at the time of the consular interview.

LOOKING AT THE GREEN CARD

The temporary green card, usually valid for six months, serves as a travel document and confers the same benefits as the permanent green card. The USCIS routinely extends temporary green cards if receipt of the permanent green card is delayed. Most interviewing USCIS offices issue the temporary green card on a letter-sized page or as an endorsed I-94 card.

The permanent green card, contains the recipient's picture, fingerprint, date of birth, date of approval and other details.

Separate interviews for family members

Green card approval includes spouses and children under 21. Circumstances often cause families to be interviewed in different places. The principal alien – the one who received green card approval – must be interviewed first and obtain approval at either a consular post or USCIS office. The applicant must instruct the interviewing office to send the approval notice and file to wherever the rest of the family will be interviewed. The receiving post will notify the family of the interview dates. These procedures (called 'Following to Join') delay the process, and there is a risk of losing the file during transfer between interviewing offices.

TRAVELLING DURING THE USCIS INTERVIEW PROCESS

Those with adjustment pending often must make frequent business trips abroad. The non immigrant visa does not expire upon filing for adjustment of status. That is, if you have a valid L-l or H-l visa, you may continue to work and travel on those visas. This however does not apply to E visas.

Most people find it simplifies processing and calendaring for them if they apply for both work and travel (advance parole) at the same time they file for adjustment. There is no work and travel documentation required for consular processing.

Note that the USCIS assumes that those who travel without advance parole have abandoned their adjustment of status petitions. Offenders must either start again, or be interviewed through consular processing. Unfortunately, the USCIS enforces this nonsensical rule. It is much better to apply for advance parole than to fight the system.

AVOIDING COMMON PITFALLS

The lack of a foreign parent company destroys the required international organisation. Multinational managers must belong to an international organisation until receipt of the green card. Don't sell or close the foreign parent company after establishing a US subsidiary. If necessary, close the company after receiving the green card.

The two-step works because it qualifies managerial transfers within an international organisation for an exemption to labour certification. Caution: The person who owns or manages a US business as an individual, rather than through an international organisation, is ineligible for the exemption from labour certification.

Labour certification requires the employer to prove that no US workers meet the job's minimum requirements. If no qualified US workers apply, the US Department of Labor (DOL) will certify the position as available to foreign workers. This process may take up to two years.

To make matters worse, the DOL will not certify self-employed people because it assumes the self-employed worker will refuse to make their job available to US workers. What business owner will fire himself when a qualified US worker appears? Self-employed people who are not multinational managers cannot use the two-step process or obtain labour certification. Self-employed people should explore the investor visa, family class or exceptional skill categories.

CONCLUSION

At present, multinational managers experience no quota wait. Also, processing and procedural issues present few problems. Proposed cuts in employment-based immigration may create future quota waits. Prior to 1990 certain multinational managers experienced one- to two-year quota waits. Today is a good time to apply for a multinational manager green card. Indeed, the timing has never been better.

THOSE WITH EXTRAORDINARY ABILITIES IN SCIENCES, ARTS AND BUSINESS

People recognised internationally as being at the top of their field qualify for this category. Celebrities, distinguished crafts people, very successful business people, winners of Nobel Prizes, or people with broad recognition in their field qualify. Since the vast majority of readers will not qualify for this position, there is no need to elaborate on this type of visa petitioner beyond mentioning that it's available. Use Forms I-140 and MA-750A and B for this category.

QUALIFYING FOR NATIONAL INTEREST EXEMPTION

Persons with exceptional ability in business, the arts or sciences, and whose skills serve American national interest, qualify for the 'national interests' exemption from labour certification. A sponsoring employer is not necessary, and the petitioner may be self-employed. 'Exceptional' means well above average but not extraordinary, as in 'extraordinary ability'. Though the USCIS only vaguely defines the term 'national interest,' the lack of detail creates an opportunity. Rather than restricting the category to, say, scientists with doctoral degrees or engineers, the USCIS invites the applicant to make a proposal.

The USCIS focuses on whether the applicant's skills serve America's national, rather than regional, interests. The applicant's skills must also be 'significant'. Although the USCIS does not define 'significant', past history suggests that Montessori school teachers, origami paper folders and other holders of interesting but non-essential skills need not apply. Recently the USCIS was ridiculed in the national press for admitting poets nobody had ever heard of, wood carvers, the local Sushi chef and the like under the national interest waiver category.

Because of the USCIS's stricter standards, I recently refused to handle a file for a young up-and-coming film producer. No problem with the chap's films, but his case won't fly for lack of a pedigree. On the other hand scientists with publications in prestigious professional journals, inventors with patents, persons with demonstrated success in business or the arts may successfully apply.

Although most cases involve aliens with advanced education, patents or other obvious qualifications (such as participation in important projects), there are enough exceptions to recommend this category to anyone with demonstrable achievements who feels their skills contribute to the artistic, economic, business or scientific interests of the US.

Persons with unique knowledge of foreign markets often qualify. Businessmen with records for turning companies around may also qualify. (Interestingly, the USCIS holds that attorneys do not qualify for this category.)

Case study

As an example of the programme's flexibility, a salmon aquaculturist with no formal training, who developed some of the first fish foods used by salmon rearing farms, was qualified under this petition. This fish food leads me to an interesting diversion. According to my applicant, salmon rearing was heavily promoted by the Norwegian government to complement mink farming. Mink food consists of fish meal and grain. The new salmon food consisted of ground mink, sans fur which went into coats, fish and grain, as well as other additives. While all this makes ecological sense and won my applicant his green card, think about it next time you eat farm raised salmon. We stressed that salmon farming is necessary in the face of declining natural salmon runs.

Combining national interest exemption with labour certification

National interest exemption may be used in tandem with labour certification. Prospective employers should apply for this category, and simultaneously start the labour certification process. If the USCIS approves the national-interest petition, stop the labour certification process. If the petition is denied, continue with labour certification. The USCIS usually responds before one is committed beyond the point of no return in the labour certification process. Remember, labour certification is the last resort, and happiness is found when cancelling that application. Use Forms I-140 and ETA 9089 for this category.

THE LAST RESORT: LABOUR CERTIFICATION

Those who don't qualify for an exemption from labour certification, read this section.

Getting the general outline

The applicant for labour certification must have an employer willing to advertise the position to prove to the Department of Labor (DOL) that no US worker meets the minimum job requirements. Quite often, after interviewing countless applicants all with credentials similar to a foreign application, the DOL determines that the foreigner is the only one who qualifies. The labour certification system tries to ensure jobs for US workers who can meet minimum job requirements.

An employer should be aware that this process may take over a year to complete. The wait can be worth it. Legal fees and the costs of advertising and other items usually run from $10,000 to $15,000, plus filing fees for the entire process, which includes labour certification, green card petition and interview.

In a typical case the applicant works for the prospective employer on an H-1B visa. Remember, H-1B visa holders generally don't qualify for the two-step. The US employer is pleased with the applicant's work and will go through the labour certification process to keep the employee. There is no requirement to work for the prospective US employer during the labour certification process; you may work abroad while the American employer files for your labour certification.

The DOL administers the labour certification process. It contracts with individual state job services or state departments of labour to provide prevailing wage.

Job requirements and prevailing wage

Labour certification means that the US DOL has determined that no available US workers meet the minimum job requirements. Upon receipt of labour certification the applicant may petition for a visa through the USCIS. Every employment-based green card applicant must go through labour certification unless they qualify for one of the exemptions previously discussed.

The employer must prove that no American workers meet the minimum job requirements at the prevailing wage. The DOL determines the minimum job requirements and prevailing wage. The employer must advertise for and try to recruit persons meeting the minimum requirements, not the most qualified persons as in a normal situation.

The salary offered to the alien must equal or exceed the prevailing wage. The prevailing wage, based on DOL surveys, reflects the wage commonly paid for similar positions in the area of intended employment. Since most employers won't hire the worst person for the job, the prevailing wage actually represents the wage employers expect to pay to the person most suitable for the job.

The labour certification process forces employers to advertise for a person who meets the minimum job requirements, while offering the wages paid to the most qualified applicants. In a normal situation, employers hire the best person for the least money, not the worst person at the salary paid to the best people. Despite the bizarre logic of this process, most labour certification petitions are successful.

Labour certification forms
The labour certification form, ETA 9089, describes the job offer for recruitment purposes. It contains fill-in blocks for the General Job Description, Education and Experience Requirements, and Special Requirements. Use this form to prove that the applicant meets the requirements of the job offered. There are different strategies for filling in the three key areas. The form may be done on-line.

Steps in the labour certification process
The labour certification process may be divided into five steps:

1. Creating the job description.

2. State employment service obtaining prevailing wage.

3. Recuitment and advertising.

4. Approval by the US DOL.

5. Filing the Immigrant Visa petition with the USCIS.

Step 1: Creating the job description
The DOL recommends minimum job qualifications. These may include the required years of experience, education levels and specific job duties. Since the DOL bases job requirements on US labour market surveys, American workers usually qualify for a job defined by the DOL. The DOL publishes the results of its surveys in the *Dictionary of Occupational Titles* and other manuals.

The onus is on the employer to convince the department that your position should include different job-related requirements from the department's standards. We generally start with the employer's actual job requirements. If the DOL objects, attempt to justify the employer's position based on the employer's past practices and business necessity. The idea is to convince the DOL that the employer based the job requirements on its normal hiring policies and did not tailor the job requirements to the applicant's skills and experience.

Sample Job Description

The following might be used as a job description for the position of a marine products market researcher.

'Develop and maintain cost accounting system. Gather, compile and analyse information from various fish processing locations, unloading docks, freight companies, *etc.* Determine costs of finished fish products. Prepare entries to the general ledger accounts. Supervise and document the flow of finished products. Jointly prepare financial statements and perform financial analyses. Provide detailed monthly profit/loss information for each fish species and interpret the data to recommend improvement and support for managerial decisions. Responsibilities also include accounts payable functions, inventory control and other accounting tasks assigned by the accounting manager. All duties performed on computer. Conduct detailed market analysis of China/Taiwan market. Develop, negotiate, service Chinese accounts. Large portion of duties performed with LOTUS software.'

Strategy

Provide as much detail as possible in a job description. Divide the job into its smallest components, as each component becomes a job requirement. The more components the greater the chance that US applicants will fail to meet a job requirement. Note the detail in the example cited.

All job requirements must have a relationship to performing the position. Be prepared to justify each job requirement. Ask yourself if you can perform the job without a particular requirement. If you can, the state Department of Labor, which reviews the job description, will strongly suggest elimination of that job requirement.

Education and Experience

The following might be used as education and experience for the marine products market researcher position.

Education. A Bachelor of Arts degree in accounting or economics required for this position.

Experience required. Job experience – 3 years; Related occupation: None.

Strategy

Employers who require more education and experience than suggested by the DOL must demonstrate the business necessity for the increased requirements. 'Business necessity' means proving that the requirement is essential to the employer's business.

For example, an employer requiring a Master's degree in accounting for a staff position, and five years' experience for an accountant, must establish a business reason for requiring the Master's degree, when most employers only require a Bachelor of Arts degree.

Because the Department of Labor bases educational and experience requirements on their job market surveys, it is difficult to deviate from their suggested requirements. Law courts tend to uphold the government job surveys. Without conducting your own job market survey, it's difficult to prove the inaccuracy of a DOL survey. On the other hand, the courts grant employers more latitude on the subject of actual job duties. For this reason it is preferable to argue about the job description and special requirements rather than the education and experience requirements.

A trap: experience gained with the petitioning employer

The applicant cannot use job-related experience gained with the petitioning employer to qualify for the job. For example, a company providing household goods moving services to Japanese customers wishes to hire a household goods movements supervisor. The applicant worked in Japan for two years as a supervisor in a household goods moving company, and worked for the prospective US employer for a year as a supervisor on an H-1B visa. The US employer normally requires three years' experience for supervisors. The applicant has two years' experience with another employer in Japan, and one year's experience with the US employer applying for the labour certification. The US employer may only require two years' experience as a supervisor, or it will exclude the applicant.

Special Requirements
The following might be used in the special requirements block for the position of marine products market researcher.

> *Special requirements.* Minimum one year experience using LOTUS software system. Two years' professional or business experience in China. Must read, write and speak fluent Mandarin Chinese. Experience may be gained concurrently. Resumé and two references required.

Strategy
The special requirements distinguish this job from similar jobs. These requirements should be tailored to the employer's business requirements, not the applicant's credentials. For example, all accountants keep books and prepare financial statements. The accountant in the example also uses a foreign accounting system and does business in a foreign language. Employers must justify all special requirements as a business necessity. 'Business necessity' means that the requirement is essential to the employer's business success.

Justify language requirements by proving that the business must be conducted in the foreign language. For example, to prove that most of the customers speak Japanese, produce business correspondence and copies of phone bills. Use common sense to justify business necessity.

An accountant who audits both a US subsidiary and the Chinese parent company must know both American and Chinese financial reporting systems. A company that recently acquired a foreign technology may require a person with experience in that technology. A company hoping to open a foreign market may need a person experienced in that market. A company providing services to foreign particular customs and habits of the foreign nationals.

Step 2: State Job Service prevailing wage
Once satisfied with the job description, the employer must send it to the appropriate State Workforce Agency (SWA).

Step 3: Recruiting
Under the new DOL Permanent Labor Certification On-Line System (PERM) regulations, which became effective March 28, 2005, there is a list of various recruitments required, one of which is with the SWA. Exactly what kind of recruitment must be done and how it must be done, will vary depending upon the position and is too detailed to outline here. Being a new process, it is still having growing pains with periodic review of the regulations.

Do not let a lawyer handle the interview. (How would you feel if you went to a job interview and faced a company lawyer?) The DOL feels the same way, and will deny the case because the interview process was unfair.

Step 4: Department of Labor approval
After completing the recruitment process, the employer must prepare Form ETA-9089 and submit either on-line or by mail to the DOL. The DOL will advise the employer of its decision. Approval is called a **Labor Certification**, meaning that the DOL has certified the job as being available to foreign workers. You may appeal denials and, quite often, the DOL lets you provide additional information to support a case.

Step 5: USCIS approval
With labour certification in hand you may file the immigrant petition with the USCIS. Use the same Form I-140 as most other employment-based petition. The filing and interview procedure is the same as for any other

work-related immigrant visa petition. Generally, the USCIS approves cases with approved labour certifications.

Occasionally, the USCIS will question an employer's ability to pay the salary of the new employee or even question the existence of the employee. To prove the ability to pay the salary, the employer must furnish tax returns and financial statements to prove it can afford to hire the new employee at the wage stated on the labour certification application.

There are people who will create a job that doesn't exist for a relative or friend. The friend or relative obtains the green card, comes to the US and goes merrily on his or her way. USCIS often makes house calls to see if the employee actually exists.

I have had to deal with several cases of over-zealous USCIS investigators. Asians often use English names for everyday use, but use their Asian names for official purposes such as the visa application. An USCIS investigator visited a small trading company in Chinatown to inquire of a Mrs Wang, Hsiao-yun. Nobody knew this person at the company, except Nancy who claimed she's one and the same. The USCIS investigator, fresh from guarding our southern borders, was not a believer. I actually had to go to court to prove that Nancy and Mrs Wang were one and the same.

The priority date
The priority date for quota-waiting begins when the labour certification application is filed with the state job service. This means applicants are not penalised by the government's snail-paced handling of the paperwork, at least for quota purposes. Although some numbers in some categories may regress from time to time.

KEEPING YOUR GREEN CARD

After going through the time, effort, expense and heartache of obtaining a green card, did you know that it can be lost without its holder doing anything wrong? This does not include the rare instances when one forfeits a green card by committing a felony or serious crime.

Once in possession of a green card you must make the US your permanent residence, meaning that you must live in the US. The USCIS often questions green card holders at ports of entry and asks when they last visited the US. If you work abroad and make only one or two short trips to the US each year, the USCIS will assume that you live abroad unless proven otherwise. If you cannot prove that you live in the US, the USCIS inspector will confiscate your green card at the port of entry and you will have to go to court to get it back.

Green card holders must prove they live in the US, while nonimmigrant visa holders must prove they don't live in the US. Living in the US means making the US your primary and permanent residence. The USCIS considers factors such as having a residence, bank account, driver's licence, credit cards, regular bills and registered vehicle, and filing US income tax returns. You do not have to own a residence; you may rent or live with a relative. The USCIS looks at all the facts and makes a judgment call as there is no clear definition of living in the US. Instead, it is a matter of facts and circumstances.

Re-entry permits

If you need to leave the US for more than six months, we recommend applying for a Permit to Re-enter. The application for this permit affords you the opportunity to explain the reason for a temporary absence from the US, and to make a formal declaration that you do not intend to relinquish your permanent US residence. You must also agree to file US income tax returns. USCIS approval gives you permission to remain abroad for up to two years, but does not guarantee re-entry.

File the Permit to Re-enter (Form I-131) at an appropriate USCIS regional processing centre. Expect a 180 or more day processing period. You must be in the US during the processing period. The USCIS will not give you permission to return to the US if you have already left. For those already abroad, there is a similar embassy procedure.

It is acceptable to explain that you were transferred abroad by your employer or that you have business abroad, and upon the conclusion of your assignment you intend to return to the US.

The re-entry permit itself is a travel document. It contains your picture along with spaces for visas and entry and exit stamps. Re-entry permits are valid for two years and may be renewed. Persons holding Taiwanese or other passports that aren't likely to be recognised often use the re-entry permit as a travel document, instead of a passport.

If you live abroad, hold a permit to re-enter and do not file income tax returns, the USCIS may confiscate your green card at a port of entry. Permission to live abroad without relinquishing a permanent US residence is conditional upon filing US income tax returns.

Remember, once you have the green card, no matter where you live, keep it until the USCIS takes it away. There is no requirement to return the green card to the USCIS. The USCIS must prove its case before your permanent residence status is lost.

Tax returns

US tax laws require green card holders and American citizens to file tax returns and report income earned anywhere in the world. Tax treaties and credits for taxes paid to foreign governments usually eliminate double taxation. Immigrants from low-tax jurisdictions should consider the tax costs of maintaining a permanent US residence. The tax dollars, in part, pay for the services that make the US a desirable place to live. There is a price for everything!

The Internal Revenue Service (IRS) and USCIS exchange information. For example, the USCIS reports all new green card approvals to the IRS, and both agencies maintain staff in foreign countries. The IRS will try to locate tax cheats; tax problems usually result in immigration problems. Although the lack of administrative resources prevents full-scale searches, random checks and tips from disgruntled citizens, personal enemies and jilted spouses often provide the USCIS and IRS with useful information.

Failure to file a tax return violates US tax laws but not immigration statutes. There is no immigration law that requires aliens to pay American taxes. However, the USCIS considers filing a tax return as important evidence of one's intention to maintain a permanent US residence. The tax issue may arise in various ways, outlined below.

CHEAP TAX PLANNING

Many people obtain green cards so that their children can attend school or live in the US. The parents are often quite content at home and have no intention of moving to America. Maintaining the green card requires filing a US tax return. If this increases your tax burden, and you don't want to live in the US, there's a simple solution – mail your green card back to the nearest Consulate or USCIS office with a letter saying you no longer wish to be a permanent resident. The children may keep their green cards because maintenance of the green card depends on the bearer, not the activities of the principal applicant. As a result your children keep their green cards and you avoid US taxes on world-wide income.

PERMITS TO RE-ENTER

The permit to re-enter form requires the applicant to promise to file US income tax returns. Failure to file may result in denial of subsequent re-entry permit applications or loss of the re-entry permit, not necessarily loss of the green card.

USCIS inspectors at ports of entry occasionally ask re-entry permit holders if they have filed US tax returns. If the answer is no, they may confiscate the re-entry permit. The USCIS inspector may also question whether the applicant has maintained a permanent US residence.

USCIS processing centres routinely ask re-entry permit

applicants if they filed US tax returns. If the answer is negative, the USCIS will deny the permit application. In this case there is little risk of losing the green card as the applicant must be present in the US to apply for the re-entry permit. It is difficult for the USCIS to revoke a green card petition when the applicant is already in the US.

Green card

A US permanent resident who lives full-time in America but does not file US income tax returns will not lose his green card, as the US is clearly his permanent residence. This person, however, may have problems with the IRS, not the USCIS.

On the other hand, a US permanent resident who lives abroad for six months or more, and fails to file tax returns, may have problems with both the IRS and USCIS. In addition to the time spent overseas, failure to file tax returns indicates that the US is not the place of permanent residence.

When tax and immigration laws conflict

Many green card holders using tax treaty elections choose to file tax returns abroad instead of in the US. Since tax treaties supersede US domestic law, one may technically make a tax treaty election without causing a problem with the IRS or USCIS. Yet immigration laws view US tax returns as important evidence of permanent residence status.

What happens when the tax and immigration laws conflict? Simply put, the American judicial system has not definitively answered this question. However, common sense suggests that if the immigration benefit is more important than avoiding US tax payments, pay the tax and don't create a fight with the USCIS. One can argue with the USCIS as a citizen without risking citizenship. But you can't argue with the USCIS as a permanent resident without risking loss of green card. Put another way, the IRS only wants to collect taxes – a matter of money – while the USCIS controls whether the individual will reside in the USA – a matter of residence. Anyone who wants to be a permanent American resident should file US income tax returns.

An example of green card forfeiture

The most common way to lose a green card is to move back to an overseas home and make only short trips to the US. This happens most often to executives, managers and business people. For example, 'Mr Smith' transfers to an overseas office while leaving his wife and children to finish school in the US. The husband commutes to visit his family. So far so good.

Mrs Smith moves to join her husband overseas, while one child stays in the US to continue schooling. The Smiths pay American income taxes but do not maintain a residence. They stay with one of their children while in the US, and their car and bills are in the child's name. Smith and his wife intend to resume living in the US once Smith retires.

During one of the Smiths' visits to their children, the USCIS questions them at the airport and learns the truth. The USCIS asks Mr Smith if he has a re-entry permit. Since Smith does not he will probably lose his green card. If Smith had had a re-entry permit he might not have experienced problems. He also should have taken a few other precautions. If he had planned correctly, the house, car and bills would have remained in his name. In other words, the child should have been living in Mr Smith's house, not the other way around.

The revocation of Mr Smith's green card does not mean that the child loses his green card. Although children may obtain green cards through parents, they do not lose green cards simply because the parents lost theirs. Adult children can petition for the parents at any time, and if the child is a citizen there is no quota wait. If Mr Smith has no other qualifying relatives in the US, he may take the matter to court or hope his company transfers him to the US again.

APPLYING FOR A SOCIAL SECURITY NUMBER

The **social security number (SSN)**, an identification number designed for social insurance purposes, has become the *de facto* national identification number. With few exceptions you need a social security number to open a bank account, apply for a loan, claim a tax deduction for dependants, apply for a credit card, obtain a driver's licence, receive a speeding ticket, buy a house, insurance and more.

Green card holders or persons with USCIS permission to work in the US may bring their USCIS documents to a social security office and apply on the spot. Dependants must prove their relationship to the working taxpayer. All others must provide proof of legal immigration status, identity, and a letter from the organisation requiring the social security number. This letter must specifically identify the applicant and state the reasons for requiring the SSN.

Non-residents of the US, and those without permission to work in the US, do not need an SSN. They may transact business in the US, such as opening a bank account, by filing a statement attesting to their non-resident status (Form W-8) or they may apply for a tax identification number (TIN) from the Internal Revenue Service.

SUMMARY

- Green card holders must make the US their primary and permanent residence.

- Tax laws, not immigration laws, require the filing of US tax returns.

- Filing tax returns is evidence of US permanent residence for immigration law purposes.

- Re-entry permits allow extended absences abroad.

- Re-entry permit holders must file US tax returns as a condition for permission to remain abroad for extended periods.

- Green cards are personal. A parent's loss of a green card does not mean the children will also lose their green cards.

10

Obtaining Student Visas

Students use F-1 visas for academic programmes and M-1 visas for vocational programmes. To be eligible for either of these visas the student must first be accepted by a school. Once the student is accepted the school will prepare Form I-20 for the student to submit to the USCIS or to a consulate. The I-20 Form provides information about the student's course of study and his or her means of financial support.

The Key difference between F-1 and M-1 is that the M-1 holders may not change to H-1B on the basis of their M-1 training. Generally, both visa categories are issued for the duration of the approved educational programme. In both cases, visa procedures may be initiated from the US or abroad.

ATTENDING PUBLIC SCHOOLS

Foreign students may only attend public (government supported) junior high schools, and high schools for 12 months plus a 60-day grace period – and then only if the student reimburses the public school for the cost of the education. Local school districts, not the state or federal government, control public education. Each school district may set its own price. There is no restriction on attending private schools.

Playing hooky

Students who drop out, work in violation of their student visa or otherwise violate the terms of their student visa, may be expelled from the US and barred from entry for five years.

FILING FOR YOUR STUDENT VISA

The procedure for obtaining an F-1 student visa is as follows:

Step 1: Be accepted by a school.

Step 2: Obtain Form I-20 from the school, officially (SEVIS Form I-20) Student and Exchange Visitor Information System. Form I-20 details the proposed course of study and estimates the financial resources necessary to complete.

Step 3: If in the US, send Form I-539 Change of Status, Form I-20 and proof of financial support to the appropriate USCIS regional processing centre. If the USCIS approves the petition, it will respond with an endorsed I-94 evidencing student status. If abroad, fill out the consular application forms, supply Form I-20 from the school as well as proof of financial support. The consul will signify approval by issuing an F-1 or M-1 visa.

TRAVELLING ON A STUDENT VISA

All students who wish to leave the US should obtain an endorsed Form I-20ID from a designated school official each time the student leaves the US. The school's endorsement proves that the student is still in school and making satisfactory progress under the approved educational programme.

Students who try to enter the US with a student visa but without an endorsed I-20ID risk denial of entry. At a minimum they must convince the USCIS at the port of entry of their intention to maintain an approved course of study.

Students may travel to Canada or Mexico for up to 30 days without a visa provided they have a valid I-94 and an endorsed I-20ID. All other overseas destinations require a visa. This means that the student who obtained student

status in the US must ultimately return home to obtain a
visa if they want to leave North America and re-enter.

PROVING FINANCIAL SUPPORT

Students must prove a source of adequate financial
support. Parents, guardians or benefactors should supply
an Affidavit of Support, Forms I-134 and I-864, and
supply proof of sufficient funds to support the student for
the duration of the approved course of study. The person
signing the Affidavit of Support guarantees that the
student will not use public assistance or welfare.
Theoretically, this is rarely enforced; the signer of the
I-134 is responsible for reimbursing the government in the
event that the student uses public assistance.

STRICT ENFORCEMENT

Since many students drop out of school, work illegally or
never attend classes, the USCIS and consuls carefully
monitor F-1 or M-1 applications. Good students attending
academically-respected institutions experience few
difficulties, but students with average or poor grades,
along with English as second-language school applicants,
experience greater scrutiny. The consuls and USCIS want
to make sure the student intends to study and not use the
student visa to disappear in the US. Students must prove
their credibility.

Where to get assistance

American schools often charge foreign students higher
tuition fees. Indeed, some schools depend on foreign
student tuition for their financial survival. Somewhere near
every major American university are residences,
dormitories or companies devoted to assisting the various
nationalities of the college's foreign students.

Although one may always consult with an attorney,
several private companies provide care and support for

foreign students and will assist with visa processing. Such companies routinely care for overseas students and often help convince the consul of a student's good standing, as well as his or her intention to study while in the US.

THREE KEY QUESTIONS, THE SAME ANSWER: YES

The consuls and USCIS ask three key questions when reviewing student visa applications. These questions, along with the recommended answers, are listed below.

1. *Do you intend to complete a full-time course of study?* Be prepared to submit past school records and letters of recommendation from teachers as evidence.

2. *Do you have financial support?* Produce proof of adequate funds and/or show the financial statement of a sponsor on Form I-134, Affidavit of Support.

3. *Will you return to your home country after your studies are completed?* Prove this intention by demonstrating close family ties in your home country and/or a network of friends, relatives or job prospects. A course of study related to a prospective job in your home country also helps indicate your plans to return. For example, a father owns a ski lodge and resort and sends his child to the US to study hotel management. In this case, the job logically relates to the course of study.

WORKING WHILE STUDYING

The following programmes allow students to work while attending a school in the US.

The programme descriptions set forth below are general in nature. They often depend on the school's policies and often change. One should ask the educational institution to describe its current offerings for employment.

On-campus employment
Any full-time student in good academic standing may work 20 hours a week at an on-campus facility during the school year and full-time between quarters or semesters. Work must be an integral part of student's educational programme.

Curricular practical training
This training must be offered in connection with a field of study. Generally, students must arrange curricular practical training with academic advisors, with the school processing the necessary paperwork. Students who work for a year or longer in this programme lose eligibility for post-completion practical training.

POST-COMPLETION PRACTICAL TRAINING PROGRAMME

This popular programme permits students to work off-campus for one year after completion of all degree requirements. Application for this programme must be made between 90 days before and 30 days after completion of a course of study. Seek the school's approval for employment. The school files the necessary forms with the USCIS.

After USCIS approval, obtain an Employment Authorisation Card (Form I-765) to work legally. File Form I-765 and go to the nearest USCIS office for photographing. The Employment Authorisation Card should be available in one or two days.

Students cannot leave the US after graduation and then apply for post-completion practical training. Practical training must be approved *before* leaving the US, and students may travel after practical training approval. Students have 60 days from the end of the practical training period to depart the US, resume studies or change to another visa status.

OPTIONS AFTER PRACTICAL TRAINING

Students hoping to stay in the US after practical training have few options. They can get married to a US citizen or find a job and apply for an H-1B or an E visa. Recent university graduates usually qualify as professionals for H-1B status. Experience is not a requirement for H-1B visa professional or speciality-worker status.

Students may qualify for E visa status if they are hired by a treaty company controlled by members of their nationality. For example, a Japanese student could obtain an E visa as a professional or manager through a Japanese-owned company.

Quite often, students and employers assume that E visas only apply to transferees from the treaty country, as when managers transfer from the home office to a US subsidiary. A treaty company may hire any qualified treaty national even if they were not previously employed by a related company abroad.

11

Visas for the Privileged, Media, Athletes, Entertainers, Cultural Exchanges, Religious Workers and Tycoons

Several lesser-used nonimmigrant visa categories deserve discussion. These include:

- I visas for persons working in information media

- O visas for outstanding artists, business people, chefs and their support staff

- P visas for professional athletes, musical groups and entertainers

- Q visas for cultural exchanges; and

- R visas for religious workers.

I VISA FOR INFORMATION MEDIA

Working for the media industry

The I visa permits employees of foreign information media engaged in news-gathering or documentary material, along with key staff such as film crews and editors, to work in the US. Independent production companies qualify as long as the journalists hold credentials issued by a journalistic association. The I visa does not require university degrees or existing US trade or business experience. The focus is on information-gathering and reporting for news or documentary purposes, not entertainment.

An example of who is eligible for the I visa might be a foreign television station that wished to send a journalist and editor to the US to collect material for documentary segments on American lifestyles. The journalist had over ten years' experience and a press card, but no university degree. The foreign television station agreed to support the journalist while in the US. This case was approved.

We have processed I visas for a radio show covering US lifestyle, a travelogue, a documentary discussion of Marilyn Monroe photos, as well as a Super Bowl play-by-play announcer. In all cases the applicants reported newsworthy events or created educational or documentary shows.

O VISA, A MINI GREEN CARD FOR OUTSTANDING ACTORS, BUSINESS PEOPLE AND ARTISTS

The O-category pertains to people with extraordinary skills. We often use the category as an alternative to H-1B for persons with no university degree. The O visa most commonly permits key actors and technical staff to work for motion picture, television and stage productions. Individual athletes, scientists, educators and tycoons may also qualify for O visas. We've used O visas for actors, artists, computer graphics designers in the television industry, and others. I'm proud to report that one of my O visa clients designed some of the commercials used during the 1997 Super Bowl telecast.

We have used O-1 visas to permit the producer, key technical staff and actors to come to Seattle, Washington, for the filming of the movie *The Little Buddha*. The producer, director, art people, cameramen and other key technicians had international experience and easily qualified for O-1 visa status. We filed O-2 petitions for the supporting actors and assistants.

O-visa applicants must obtain letters from an industry's professional organisation and a labour organisation attesting to their outstanding qualifications. It must be stated that there is no objection to granting a visa to the aliens. Unions often resist providing favourable letters if they believe qualified American workers exist.

The O visa may be issued for an initial validity period of three years with extensions of one year each thereafter. The O visas can be extended indefinitely, a mini green card, as long as the applicant retains his or her preeminence.

The O visa category can be used by just about anyone who is famous or internationally acclaimed in a recognised field of endeavour. Consider this category when the visa candidate does not have a university degree. Remember, the applicant must either be famous or possess esoteric skills. Otherwise, labour unions won't issue favourable advisory opinions.

WORKING AS AN ATHLETE OR ENTERTAINER

The P visa works, as a practical matter, the same as the O visa except that it applies to athletes and entertainment groups. For example, a Bunraku or Japanese puppet troupe would use P visas for the puppeteers, readers and key support staff. P visas also apply to athletic teams, boxers, sumo wrestlers and ethnic dance troupes. Validity periods depend on the length of the engagements, not to exceed five years or ten years for athletes.

Q VISA FOR CULTURAL EXCHANGE PROGRAMMES

Q visas are for cultural exchange programmes which provide a sharing of history, culture or traditions of the alien's country of nationality. The Q visa cultural exchange programme must be designed to exhibit the history, culture, religion, attitudes, philosophy or traditions of the alien's home country. The alien's employment must be connected to making the cultural exchange programme work. One of our Q visa cases was a programme hosted by an Indian restaurant that exhibited the traditions, philosophy and preparation of regional Indian cooking. The Indian restaurant used a Q visa to hire a chef to run

the programme. Validity periods depend on the length of
the engagements, generally not to exceed 15 months.

R VISA FOR RELIGIOUS WORKERS

At least some members of virtually every ethnic group in
the world live in the US. Consider that members of any
particular ethnic group divide their loyalties among several
different religions. Some religions have nothing to do with
ethnic affiliation, while others cater to a particular ethnic
group.

For example, in Seattle, Washington, there is a Finnish
Lutheran Church, a Swedish Lutheran Church and many
other non-ethnic Lutheran churches. While all are
Lutherans, there is a special church council or governing
body for the Finns and another for the Swedes. The Finns
and Swedes prefer ministers who speak the native
language and are trained in native customs. Many other
churches, temples and synagogues have the same
preference. The R visa for religious occupations satisfies
this purpose.

Religious institutions catering to a particular ethnic
group often make that group's members more comfortable
by providing a minister or religious workers from the
home country to perform services and other religious and
cultural activities.

Ministers

Ministers must be authorised to conduct religious services
for the specific denomination, and must have at least a US
baccalaureate degree or foreign equivalent as well as have
been a member of the religious organisation for at least two
years prior to applying. Apply through the USCIS
application, or application can be made directly to the consul
by letter. The visa is usually valid for three years with a two-
year extension. The R visa is very flexible and available to all
religions. There is also a green card category available to
religious workers. The requirements are very similar to the R
visa, and religious workers are exempt from labour
certification.

I never gave this category much thought until a few
years ago when we helped Buddhist nuns from Taiwan. I
assumed that any woman who shaved her head, wore a
nondescript saffron robe, and bore ritual tattoos and burn
marks could be considered a legitimate Buddhist. I was
wrong. The USCIS gently informed me that Taiwanese
and Thai businessmen and women, in particular, often give
large donations to a temple, disguise themselves as monks
or nuns, and apply for an R visa and then a green card as
a religious worker. Very clever. This is an abused
category, so be prepared to carefully document your
religious convictions and affiliation. The more strict
consuls require ritual by fire.

When a pastor of the Finnish Lutheran Church in
Seattle passed away the church members wanted a Finnish
replacement. The new replacement was ordained by the
governing body of the church, studied religion at
university level, and had over two years' experience. The
church is a nonprofit religious organisation. This case
more than met the legal requirements for an R visa.

Religious workers

Another case arose when a religious outreach programme,
again Lutheran, needed a social worker to direct a
programme to help refugees from Somalia, Eritrea and
Ethiopia. The refugees were having trouble adjusting to
life in the US, and the church-sponsored outreach
programme provided social and religious counselling
services as well as religious training. The programme did
not require a minister but needed a social worker with
Lutheran training.

The applicant had a nursing degree plus two years of
religious training and over two years' experience providing
religious comfort to sick people in Lutheran hospitals in
Finland. The applicant had worked for a Lutheran hospital
for over two years. This applicant's credentials exceeded
the minimum requirements.

R visa religious workers may include counsellors, social
workers, health-care workers for religious hospitals,

missionaries, translators, religious broadcasters and just about any other occupation necessary to a religious organisation. The term 'religious worker' does not include janitors, fund raisers and people removed from the religion. An exception to this is seen in the few religions where the janitor must follow religious practices.

DETAILS ABOUT NAFTA

The North American Free Trade Agreement (NAFTA) provides additional nonimmigrant visa categories mostly for professional workers (Treaty Nationals, designated TN) for citizens of Mexico and Canada to work in the US. The reverse applies for US citizens wishing to work in Mexico or Canada. The complete list of NAFTA categories is available from the US, Canadian or Mexico consulates. The list is also available in the Federal Register, Site 8C.F.R., Section 214.6 (c).

Additionally under NAFTA, Canadians may apply for L-1 status at specified land border crossings or airports. Mexicans must continue to apply through USCIS regional processing centres. For Canadians the NAFTA filing procedures avoid processing delays incurred at USCIS regional processing centres.

Expedited procedures for Canadians under NAFTA
Canadian TN applicants may apply at land border ports of entry and designated airports. Applications simply consist of an employer letter explaining eligibility for the particular category and documented proof, such as university transcripts or verification of required experience. No additional forms are necessary. Border processing usually occurs on the spot. The USCIS evidences Treaty National status by issuing an I-94 card endorsed 'TN'.

All Treaty Nationals may work in the US for periods of up to one year, and TN status may be renewed annually. Although NAFTA does not limit the number of extensions available to TN visa holders, common sense dictates that the USCIS will question frequent extension applicants.

Strategy

The NAFTA visas afford Canadians fast processing with minimal paperwork when the system works. Processing procedures and policies vary among the border-crossing posts. Enforcement policies also vary; some posts are stricter than others. Since the situation constantly changes, we advise NAFTA applicants to check for local procedures before applying at a border post.

Most NAFTA applicants also qualify for H, L or E visa status. NAFTA works for those who wish to work in the US for a short period of time, or for those who need to quickly start work in America. Once in the US, NAFTA applicants may change to a longer-term nonimmigrant visa, such as H-1, E-1/2 or L-1A.

It is important to note that all NAFTA visas automatically expire upon application for labour certification or permanent residence. Because NAFTA visas only last one year and permanent residence processing takes more than one year, it is important to change from a NAFTA status to another non immigrant status that lasts more than one year, such as E, H, or L, before applying for permanent residence status. Otherwise, the NAFTA visa holder will find themselves out of status in the US, out of job in the US and must return to Canada to wait for the permanent residence visa to be approved.

SELF ASSESSMENT

Nonimmigrant visas

- You are taking a trip for business or pleasure: use visa waiver. If the trip exceeds 90 days or you do not qualify for visa waiver: use B-1/2.

- You have a university degree: you may qualify for H-1B if you can find a job.

- You have unique skills or outstanding accomplishments: use O-1; and if you have a university degree O-1 or H-1B.

- You work for a multinational company in a managerial position: L-1A or E-1/2. If you also have a university degree: H-1B.

- You own your own company and want to set up a US operation: as above.

- You don't own your own company and you want to make a US investment: consider E-2.

- You don't own your own company and you want to import or export goods or services from the US: consider E-1.

- None of the above applies, but no US worker meets the minimum job requirements: H-2.

Green cards

- You marry a US citizen or have US parents: immediate relative.

- You have US permanent resident spouse or parents: 2nd preference but be prepared to wait at least two years.

- You have US citizen brothers or sisters: 4th preference but be prepared to wait.

- You work for a multinational corporation as a manager or higher: multi-national manager, one of the simplest ways to get a green card.

- You have extraordinary skills: pass Go, collect $200.

- You have exceptional skills in US national interests: national interest waiver.

- You are an outstanding researcher at an academic or research institution: let your employer take care of the visa processing.

- None of the above: you must go through labour certification or invest at least $500,000.

12

Naturalisation: Becoming an American Citizen

Most countries of the world base citizenship on parentage, and try to limit citizenship to particular ethnic heritage. For example, a person born in Japan or France must have a Japanese or French parent to become a citizen. Many countries require a male qualifying parent, while a few nations require a female qualifying parent. Recently, many countries have eliminated the sex discrimination but retained the parentage requirement.

America, a country open to all ethnic groups, automatically grants citizenship to any person born in the US, regardless of parental nationality and why or how long the parents were in the country. Persons born in America merely need to present a birth certificate to apply for a passport. Otherwise, US citizenship, with few exceptions, requires the passage of time as a green card resident, basic knowledge of US history and government, and an ability to speak English.

Because many people plan to give birth to a child in the US (for automatic citizenship), there is some talk about requiring a greater than nine-month residency requirement. This is known in the trade as 'baby droppers'.

LITERACY REQUIREMENT

In order to be naturalised all applicants must demonstrate their ability to read, write, understand, and speak the English language. The exceptions are persons who are 50 years of age and over who have been permanent residents in the US, for a minimum of 20 years, or, persons who are 55 years of age and have been permanent residents in the US, for a minimum of 15 years.

CIVICS REQUIREMENT

No applicant shall be naturalised who cannot demonstrate a knowledge and understanding of the fundamentals of the history, principles, and form of government of the United States. There are no exemptions from this requirement.

ADVANTAGES OF CITIZENSHIP

There are two practical advantages of US citizenship: You can vote, and it's hard to lose citizen status. You can lose citizenship if you lied to get a green card, failed to disclose past crimes, or perjured a material fact relating to citizenship or a green card. Unlike aliens who can lose their green card as a result of prolonged absence from the US, American citizens may leave the country and return at any time without fear of losing citizenship.

Every American citizen can vote. Since permanent residents are taxpayers, they want to have a say about the amount of income tax and how it's spent. There are many other important reasons to vote.

DUAL CITIZENSHIP

The US permits dual nationality. American citizens of dual nationality must consult the other country about holding two passports. The US government does not inquire or even care if a person owns two passports. For example, a US citizen holding US and Japanese passports may risk losing his Japanese passport to the Japanese government, but not the US passport.

THE QUALIFYING PERIOD

A green card spouse of a US citizen must reside in the US for three years before becoming eligible for citizenship. All other permanent residents must reside in the US for five years. If your American spouse dies while you have a green card, you still may qualify under the three-year rule.

You must live in the U.S. for 50 per cent of the three or five year qualifying period. One may apply for citizenship three months prior to the end of the qualifying period. A break in residence between six months and one year may distrupt the qualifying residence period unless the applicant can prove the US was his primary residence. Proof consists of US tax returns, US employment, US property etc. A break in residency of one year or more requires the applicant to satisfy the residency period by waiting for four years and one day to file for naturalisation. One should obtain a permit to re-enter to prevent breaks in residency. Even so, time spent abroad with the permit to re-enter does not count toward the residency requirements.

THE CITIZENSHIP TEST

Upon meeting the residency requirements, you may file for naturalisation at any USCIS District Office. File the appropriate form (N-400), which includes biographical information and proof of required residence. The USCIS will schedule an interview for the person to be tested on US history and government. Only those who meet the literacy requirement exemptions will avoid being tested in English.

The test questions are the same sorts of things most Americans learn in junior high school. Several books are available in libraries and book stores to provide sample questions and study aids. Most immigration examiners ask reasonable questions. Examiners tend to ask difficult questions when they suspect the applicant did not study. Sample questions could include:

'Do you know how many congressmen comprise the Senate and House of Representatives?'

'Can you name the first five Presidents in order?'

'Do you know who was the President of the Confederacy?'

USCIS examiners tend to be understanding of those who studied for the test. When asked, 'Who was George Washington?' one of my clients answered, 'My first son.' Confused, the elderly woman, with help from the USCIS examiner, managed to regain her composure and pass the test. In another case a young Chinese woman, laden with gold jewellery and who obviously didn't study, was rejected after she failed to identify the metal responsible for the California Gold Rush. (By the way, the Chinese characters for San Francisco translate to 'Gold Mountain'.) This woman had made no attempt to learn English and the examiner was looking for a way for her to fail the test.

OBTAINING A CERTIFICATE OF NATURALISATION

Upon passing the citizenship test and residency requirements, a citizenship paper (called the 'Certificate of Naturalisation') can be obtained from the USCIS or a federal court. Name changes are permissible at the time of naturalisation, if so desired.

The USCIS procedure is faster. The federal court procedure, scheduled every few months, is more elaborate. In the court procedure the judge says a few kind words, the citizenship candidates pledge allegiance to the US, and they then receive naturalisation certificates.

Many people prefer the more elaborate federal court ceremony to commemorate this important event. On the 4th of July, Independence Day in the US, most American cities hold a large citizenship ceremony. People from all over the world, with different backgrounds, experience and personal stories of how they came to the US, become American citizens at the same time. We call this American phenomenon the 'melting pot', whereby people from all over the world become citizens of the United States of America.

PRACTICAL POINTERS FOR NATURALISATION APPLICANTS

- You can file three months before you are technically eligible.

- You must live in the USCIS district where you file for the three-month period prior to filing.

- Expect the process to take a year, often longer.

- Lawyers can't make the process faster.

- The USCIS often tries to use naturalisation as a lever to entice tax cheats to pay up. This practice is actually against the law. As a practical matter, it's better to pay up than experience significant delays in processing while you argue about your rights.

- There are expedited procedures for military personnel.

13

Thoughts for Human Resource Managers and Employees

Overseas relocation requires consideration of the needs of the family, not just the employee. Changes in life style, education, environment and career can disrupt seemingly stable families. Employees often feel they must choose between the commitment to their careers and to their families.

The employee's willingness to relocate, and their future job performance, can be affected by damaged family relationships caused by a spouse having to give up a career, unsettled children who cannot cope at schools, the elderly relatives left behind. Why take a risk on moving? It's not just a matter of career and remuneration.

Many employees and their families find overseas relocation frustrating and difficult. The amount of information and advice required for a smooth transition can be overwhelming. Inaccurate advice may result in ill will towards the employer.

The HR professional must not only sell the concept of moving for positive reasons, but also ensure a smooth landing for the entire family. Despite the risks and expenses, overseas assignments will dramatically increase in years to come as the rate of business globalisation increases.

WHY SEND AN EMPLOYEE OVERSEAS?

The expatriate may:

- Act as a representative of the parent company, responsible for the whole business, which demands an extensive range of management skills that would not be learned at home.

- Be responsible for maintaining the corporate culture and control over newly created or acquired subsidiaries.

- Alleviate a shortage of specialised skills not available locally.

- Act as a liaison between the head office and the foreign subsidiary.

- Enable the company to maintain its identity and serve their own nationals. For example, the Japanese airline needs to employ mostly Japanese crews so that they can communicate and serve their Japanese customers better.

UNDERSTANDING WHY EMPLOYEES WANT TO GO ABROAD

The successful HR manager creates excitement around the opportunity to live and work abroad. They promote the 'good' reasons to move rather than threaten the employee with retribution if he refuses to relocate.

Many employees see relocation as a personal challenge; some view it as a professional opportunity, some take the chance because of a higher salary and some may want to experience other cultures. There are also those who are fed up with the management style at home or see this opportunity as a fresh start or the only way of progressing. Some view it as a chance to send their children to top schools at company expense. The expatriate can enjoy the best of the host country without worrying about living there forever.

EASING THE TRANSITION TO OVERSEAS LIFE

Manning a foreign post can be a lonely and stressful task for some, an opportunity for others. The reaction of family members may influence the relocated employee's job performance. The transition to overseas life works smoothly when the family unit makes a happy landing abroad.

Information and support are key to easing the transition to overseas life. Avoid conflict that can interfere with employees' productivity and corporate objectives by listening and responding to employees' needs, however mundane, at the beginning of the transfer. Encourage employees and their families to maintain a sense of control over the process by:

1   Providing adequate information.
2   Providing approachable communication.
3   Taking a flexible approach to service provision.

Explaining important differences

The US state and Federal governments, compared with most industrial countries, provide a minimum of social services. Many relocated employees are surprised by how much they must do for themselves. Although this system tends to keep taxes lower, the uninitiated must be prepared.

Remember, the USA does not provide national health insurance. The countless variations among company health plans, preferred provider organisations, health maintenance organisations, co-operative health organisations, fee for service health plans, all require explanation.

Drunk driving laws require attention. Most US cities do not have adequate public transport. This means you must drive home from the pub or party. In most states the alcohol limit is .08, or two beers. The penalty is usually suspension of the driver's licence, plus a fine. As a result car insurance, all privately provided, will become prohibitively expensive or nonexistent.

It is useful to provide a list of favourite food stores, restaurants and pubs, a referral to a local lawyer and accountant, tips on local idiosyncrasies, and driver licence information. The employee is starting again; the HR professional must assist in the process or the employee will spend too much time adjusting rather than working.

Working spouses

The needs of spouses have become a major issue. Relocation packages should account for the needs of dual career couples. Relocation can put an immense strain on a relationship. However, it has recently become possible for the spouses of L-1 and E-1 and E-2 visa holders to obtain work authorisation, relieving much of the strain. Obtaining work authorisation for a non immigrant spouse is done by filing form I-765 with proof of status, with the service center of jurisdiction. There is no restriction on the type of employment the non immigrant spouse may seek.

RELOCATION TIPS FOR COMPANY EMPLOYEES AND INDIVIDUALS

Ask lots of questions. For example:

- How flexible is the relocation package?
- What provisions are there for keeping the family together during the relocation?
- Who will talk to my partner?
- What happens if I can't sell my house?
- How much time do I have to look for a new home?
- To what extent can I control the timing of the move?
- Can you arrange a working visa for my spouse?
- Where will my children go to school, and who pays?
- What personal belongings may I bring without customs duty?
- Can I ship my car or should I buy a new one?
- Who will provide health insurance?
- What company relocation allowances are available?
- Who pays moving and travel costs?
- Who takes on the risks of currency fluctuations?

- Will an acceptable position be waiting when I return?

- Will time abroad count towards company retirement benefits?

Preparing for everyday differences
Then there are all the mundane questions ranging from the local electrical current, to the location of the dry cleaners.

Some easy answers to the above. You can bring household effects to the USA duty free. Don't ship the car because foreign cars must be fitted with expensive, performance reducing pollution control devices. Most foreign household appliances, particularly CD players, don't work well on US current even with an adaptor.

Try to learn about US cultural differences before leaving home. The US is a big country. There are regional cultural differences. There is an American–UK or other country chamber of commerce chapter in most US and foreign major cities. These organisations often provide social contacts and help with the particulars of living in the USA.

Planning your return
Whether you come to the US as an individual investor or employee, plan an exit strategy. Repatriation can be as hard as adjusting to overseas life. The world did not stop just because you moved overseas. Be prepared to make new friends, get used to the new work environment and, probably, a new boss and position.

International relocation becomes more common every day. Since the costs of relocating in both human and financial terms are very high, preparation is necessary to get the process right.

Appendix 1
Immigration Forms and Other Documents

FORMS REQUIRING NO FILING FEES

The following forms require no filing fees. Forms are available from the US Government Printing Office or a local USCIS office.

Form number	Title
ETA 750 parts A and B	Application for Labor Certification
ETA-9035	Labor condition application (part of H-1B filing)
G-325	Biographical (usually used in the US only)
I-9	Confirmation of Authority to Work
DS-156	Visa Application/Revalidation
DS-179	Document Checklist (Embassy)
DS-230 parts 1 and 2	Biographical (Embassy)
DS-1–134	Affidavit of Support (for employment-based applicants)
I-864	Affidavit of Support (for family-class applicants) and some employment-based if beneficiary is 5 per cent or more owner
AR-11	Alien's change of address form

FORMS REQUIRING FEES

Since filing fees change frequently, they will not be included in this book. For an updated Fee List contact an USCIS centre.

Form number	Title
I-17	Petition for Approval of School for Attendance by Nonimmigrant Students
I-90	Application to Replace Alien Registration Card

I-102	Application for Replacement/Initial Nonimmigrant Arrival-Departure Document
I-129	Petition for Nonimmigrant Worker
I-129E	Supplement for E Visa
I-129F	Petition for Alien Fiancé(e)
I-129H	Supplement for H Visas
I-129L	Supplement for L Visas
I-130	Petition for Alien Relative
I-131	Application for Travel Document/Request for Advance Parole
I-140	Petition for Prospective Immigrant Employee
I-191	Application for Advance Permission to Return to Unrelinquished Domicile
I-192	Application for Advanced Permission to Enter as Nonimmigrant
I-193	Application for Waiver of Passport and/or Visa
I-212	Application for Permission to Reapply for Admission into the United States After Deportation or Removal
I-246	Application for Stay of Deportation
I-290B	Notice of Appeal to the Administrative Appeal Unit
I-360	Petition for Amerasian, Widow(er), or Special Immigrant (except there is no fee for a petition seeking classification as an Amerasian)
I-485	Application for Permanent Residence
I-526	Immigrant Petition by Alien Entrepreneur
I-539	Application to Extend/Change Nonimmigrant Status
I-600	Petition to Classify Orphan as an Immediate Relative
I-600A	Application for Advance Processing of Orphan Petition
I-601	Application for Waiver of Grounds of Excludability
I-612	Application for Waiver of the Foreign Residence Requirement
I-690	Application for Waiver of Grounds of Excludability (replaced by I-601)
I-694	Notice of Appeal of Decision under

	Section 210 or 245A of the Immigration and Nationality Act
I-695	Application for Replacement of Form I-688A, Employment Authorization for Form I-688, Temporary Residence Card
I-698	Application to Adjust Status from Temporary to Permanent Resident
I-751	Petition to Remove the Conditions of Residence
I-765	Application for Employment Authorization
I-817	Application for Voluntary Departure Under the Family Unity Program
I-821	Application for Temporary Protected Status
I-823	Application for Alternative Inspection Service
I-824	Application for Action on an Approval Application or Petition
I-907	Request for Premium Processing
Motions	Motions to Reopen or Reconsider
N-300	Application to File Declaration of Intention
N-336	Request for Hearing on a Decision Naturalization Processing
N-400	Application for Naturalization
N-410	Motion for Amendment of Petition (Application)
N-455	Application for Transfer of Petition for Naturalization
N-470	Application to Preserve Residence for Naturalization Purposes
N-565	Application for Replacement Naturalization Purposes
N-600	Application for Certificate of Citizenship
N-643	Application for Certificate of Citizenship on Behalf of an Adopted Child
N-644	Application for Posthumous Citizenship

Appendix 2
Visa Categories

NONIMMIGRANT VISA CATEGORIES

Here is a list of virtually all of the nonimmigrant visa categories. Some of the lesser used categories have been combined into one description. All visa categories are designated by letters of the alphabet. Subcategories are designated by numbers. For example, L is the letter designating visas for international organisations. L-1 is for the principal applicant, L-2 is for dependants.
'Dependants' means spouse and children under 21 years of age.

A-1 to A-3   Diplomats, public ministers, dependants and personal attendants.

B-1   Business visitors.

B-2   Tourist visitors.

C-1   Travellers in transit through the US.

D-1   Airline or ship crew.

E-1   Treaty trader.

E-2   Treaty investor.

F-1   Academic and language training students.

G-1 to G-5   Representatives of foreign governments and employers of quasi-governmental international organisations and some United Nations employees, servants and dependants.

NATO-1 to
NATO-5   Certain employees and military personnel of the North Atlantic Treaty Organisation, dependants and servants.

H-1C   Registered nurses.

H-1B	Speciality occupations and professionals.
H-2A	Temporary or seasonal agricultural workers unavailable in the US.
H-2B	Other temporary or seasonal workers unavailable in the US.
H-3	Temporary trainees learning skills unavailable in their home country; Special Education Exchange Program
H-4	Immediate family of H visa classifications.
I	Foreign press and information media coming to report on newsworthy or informational events as opposed to selling entertainment.
J-1	Exchange visitors coming as part of a Department of State-approved exchange programme.
J-2	Dependants of J visa holders.
K-1	Fiancé(e)s of US citizens who intend to marry within 90 days of entry.
K-2	Dependant of K-1
K-3	Spouse of USC (US citizen)
K-4	Dependant of K-3
L-1	Intra-company transferees in an executive, managerial or specialised knowledge capacity.
L-2	L-1 dependants.
M-1	Vocational school students.
M-2	M-1 dependants.
N-1	Certain parents and children of special immigrants.
O-1	Individuals of extraordinary ability in the arts, sciences, business, professions or athletics.
O-2	Essential support staff of O-1 aliens.
O-3	O visa dependants.
P-1	Internationally-renowned artists, athletes and entertainers and their support staff.
P-2	Entertainers coming to perform at a government approved cultural exchange programme.
P-3	Culturally-unique entertainers.

P-4	P visa dependants.
Q-1	Participants in international cultural exchange programmes; may be privately sponsored.
Q-2	Q visa dependants.
R-1	Ministers and religious workers.
R-2	R visa dependants.
S	International terrorist informants.
V	Spouse of US permanent resident who have already waited three years for their priority date can come to the US to join their US spouse.
TN	North American Free Trade Agreement (NAFTA) nationals.

PERMANENT RESIDENT VISA CATEGORIES

Family Sponsored Preferences

Immediate Relative: Spouses, parents, and unmarried children under the age of 21, of US citizens. There is no quota wait for this category.

Second Preference: Unmarried sons and daughters of US citizens.

Third Preference: Spouses and children, and unmarried sons and daughters of permanent residents.

Fourth Preference: Married sons and daughters of US citizens.

Fifth Preference: Brothers and sisters of adult US citizens.

Employment-Based Preferences

First Preference: Priority workers, international managers.

Second Preference: Members of professions holding advanced degrees or persons of exceptional ability.

Third Preference: Skilled workers, professionals and other workers.

Fourth Preference: Certain special immigrants.

Fifth Preference: Employment creation.

Appendix 3
Important Addresses

US CITIZENSHIP AND IMMIGRATION SERVICE CENTRES

Vermont

The Vermont CIS Service Centre has jurisdiction over the following states: Massachusetts, Connecticut, New Hampshire, Rhode Island, New York, Pennsylvania, Delaware, Washington D.C., West Virginia, Maryland, New Jersey, Virginia, Maine and Vermont.

It also has jurisdiction over the following USCIS offices: Puerto Rico, Bermuda, Toronto, Montreal, Virgin Islands and Dominican Republic.

Vermont Service Centre
Citizenship and Immigration Service
75 Lower Welden Street
St Albans, VT 05479-0001
Tel: (802) 527-4913

Nebraska

The Nebraska USCIS Service Centre has jurisdiction over the following states: Michigan, Illinois, Indiana, Wisconsin, Oregon, Alaska, Minnesota, North Dakota, South Dakota, Kansas, Missouri, Washington, Idaho, Colorado, Utah, Wyoming, Ohio, Nebraska, Iowa and Montana.

It also has jurisdiction over the following USCIS offices: Manitoba, British Columbia and Calgary.

Nebraska Service Centre
Bureau of Citizenship and Immigration Service
850 'S' Street
Lincoln, NE 68501

Texas
The Texas USCIS Service Centre has jurisdiction over the following states: Florida, Texas, New Mexico, Oklahoma, Georgia, North Carolina, South Carolina, Alabama, Louisiana, Arkansas, Mississippi, Tennessee and Kentucky.

It also has jurisdiction over the following USCIS offices: Bahamas, Freeport and Nassau.

Texas Service Centre
Citizenship and Immigration Service
4141 St. Augustine Road
Dallas, TX 75337
Tel: (214) 381-1423

California
The California USCIS Service Centre has jurisdiction over the following states and territory: California, Hawaii, Arizona, Nevada and Guam.

California Service Centre
Citizenship and Immigration Service
24000 Avila Road
2nd Floor, Room 2302
Laguna Niguel, CA 92677

CONSULATES
Each foreign country has its own consular office. Look in your local telephone directory for the consulate nearest you.

VISA OFFICE

US Visa Office
2401 E Street N.W.
Washington, D.C. 20522–0106

Appendix 4
Suggested Document Lists

Below are the suggested document lists for the various visa applications. The documents listed are necessary for background information for a particular visa petition. Note that your case may require additional information.

E-1 TREATY TRADER VISA APPLICATION
1. Information concerning parent company
a. Articles of Incorporation, seal page only.
b. Financial Statement.
c. Company brochure and general description of business.
d. Organisational chart, number of employees and general job titles.
e. Business goal in the US.
f. Shareholders, percent ownership and nationality.
g. In case of holding companies, supply description of business activities of principal investors or shareholders.

2. Information concerning the US company or enterprise
a. Articles of Incorporation and organisational documents.
b. Financial Statement and Pro Forma for start-up.
c. Description of business goals in the US.
d. US organisational chart and staffing requirements.
e. Evidence of initial and continuing investment: *ie,* currency transfers and invoices.
f. Job description of transferee.
g. Amount and proof of trade between the US and foreign company; *ie,* invoices, shipping document samples, in-house accounting, computer, *etc.*
h. Proof of US investment, trade activities, currency transfers, *etc.*

3. Information concerning the alien

a. Personal data, name, date of birth, address in foreign country in last two years.
b. Resumé detailing complete employment history with salaries for recent jobs.
c. Educational history.
d. Biographical details regarding accompanying family members, if any.

E-2 TREATY INVESTOR VISA APPLICATION

1. Information concerning parent company

a. Articles of Incorporation, seal page only.
b. Financial Statement.
c. Company brochure and general description of business.
d. Organisational chart, number of employees and general job titles.
e. Corporate ownership of parent company; documents substantiating each tier of ownership, *ie*, trusts or holding companies. Stock registers and the first page of the organisational documents of each entity generally suffice. Copies of passports for each shareholder.

2. Information concerning the US company or enterprise

a. Articles of Incorporation, first page only.
b. Financial Statement.
c. Description of business, business plan, Pro Forma financial statement.
d. US organisational chart.
e. Lease or proof of ownership of US premises.
f. Job descriptions.
g. Amount of capital invested in US business; documents evidencing transfer of funds from parent company to US subsidiary and application of funds.
h. Proof of ownership of US company, *ie* stock register.

3. Information concerning the alien
a. Personal data, name, date and place of birth, address in foreign company.
b. Resumé detailing employment history and salaries.
c. Educational history.
d. Details regarding accompanying family members, if any.

H-1 PROFESSIONAL VISA APPLICATION

1. Information concerning the employee
a. University degree(s).
b. Complete resumé with date and place of birth, home address abroad, address in the US, list of prior employers with your job description at each place of employment.
c. Your salary with US employer.

2. Information about the US employer
a. Articles of Incorporation for the US employer.
b. Gross and net annual income of the US employer; if company is a start-up, send a Pro Forma financial statement.
c. Brochure, if any, for US employer or its corporate group.

L-1 (INTRA-COMPANY TRANSFEREES IN AN EXECUTIVE, MANAGERIAL OR SPECIALISED KNOWLEDGE CAPACITY) VISA APPLICATION

I. Information concerning the parent company
a. Articles of Incorporation.
b. Financial Statement.
c. Company brochure and general description of business.
d. Organisational chart, number of employees and general job titles.
c. Corporate ownership of parent company; documents substantiating each tier of ownership, ie, trusts or holding companies. Stock registers and the first page of the organisational documents of each entity generally suffice. Copies of passports for each shareholder.

2. Information concerning the US company or enterprise

a. Articles of Incorporation and organisational documents.

b. Pro Forma financial statement.

c. Description of business.

d. Proposed US organisational chart.

e. Lease or proof of ownership of US premises.

f. Applicant's job description.

g. Amount of capital invested in US business; documents evidencing transfer of funds from parent company to US subsidiary.

h. Proof of ownership of US company, *ie*, stock register.

i. Federal tax identification number.

3. Information concerning the alien

a. Personal data; name, date and place of birth, address in foreign company.

b. Resumé detailing employment history and salary for most recent position and last residence address(es).

c. Educational history.

d. Details regarding accompanying family members, if any.

Appendix 5
Typical Citizenship Questions

DEPARTMENT OF JUSTICE, IMMIGRATION AND NATURALIZATION SERVICE: 100 TYPICAL QUESTIONS

1. What are the colours of our flag?
2. How many stars are there in our flag?
3. What colour are the stars on our flag?
4. What do the stars on the flag mean?
5. How many stripes are there in the flag?
6. What colour are the stripes?
7. What do the stripes on the flag mean?
8. How many states are there in the Union?
9. What is the 4th of July?
10. What is the date of Independence Day?
11. Independence from whom?
12. What country did we fight during the Revolutionary War?
13. Who was the first President of the United States?
14. Who is the President of the United States today?
15. Who is the Vice-President of the United States today?
16. Who elects the President of the United States?
17. Who becomes President of the United States if the President should die?
18. For how long do we elect the President?
19. What is the Constitution?
20. Can the Constitution be changed?
21. What do we call changes to the Constitution?
22. How many changes or amendments are there to the Constitution?
23. How many branches are there in our government?
24. What are the three branches of our government?
25. What is the Legislative branch of our government?
26. Who makes the laws in the United States?

27. What is Congress?
28. What are the duties of Congress?
29. Who elects Congress?
30. How many senators are there in Congress?
31. Can you name the two senators from your State?
32. For how long do we elect each senator?
33. How many representatives are there in Congress?
34. For how long do we elect the representatives?
35. What is the Executive branch of our government?
36. What is the Judiciary branch of our government?
37. What are the duties of the Supreme Court?
38. What is the supreme law of the United States?
39. What is the Bill of Rights?
40. What is the capital of your State?
41. Who is the current governor of your State?
42. Who becomes President of the US if the President and the Vice-President should die?
43. Who is the Chief Justice of the Supreme Court?
44. Can you name the 13 original states?
45. Who said, 'Give me liberty or give me death'?
46. Which countries were our enemies during World War II?
47. What are the 49th and 50th states of the union?
48. How many terms can a President serve?
49. Who was Martin Luther King, Jr.?
50. Who is the head of your local government?
51. According to the Constitution, a person must meet certain requirements in order to be eligible to become President. Name one of these requirements.
52. Why are there 100 senators in the Senate?
53. Who selects the Supreme Court Justices?
54. How many Supreme Court Justices are there?
55. Why did the Pilgrims come to America?
56. What is the head executive of a state government called?
57. What is the head executive of a city government called?
58. What holiday was celebrated for the first time by the American Colonists?
59. Who was the main writer of the Declaration of Independence?
60. When was the Declaration of Independence adopted?
61. What is the basic belief of the Declaration of Independence?
62. What is the National Anthem of the United States?

63. Who wrote *The Star-Spangled Banner*?
64. Where does freedom of speech come from?
65. What is the minimum voting age in the United States?
66. Who signs Bills into law?
67. What is the highest court in the United States?
68. Who was the President during the Civil War?
69. What did the Emancipation Proclamation do?
70. What special group advises the President?
71. Which President is called the 'Father of our Country'?
72. What Immigration and Naturalization Service form is used to apply to become a naturalized citizen?
73. Who helped the Pilgrims in America?
74. What is the name of the ship that brought the Pilgrims to America?
75. What were the 13 original States of the United States called?
76. Name three rights or freedoms guaranteed by the Bill of Rights.
77. Who has the Power to Declare War?
78. What kind of government does the United States have?
79. Which President freed the slaves?
80. In what year was the Constitution written?
81. What are the first ten amendments to the Constitution called?
82. Name one purpose of the United Nations.
83. Where does Congress meet?
84. Whose rights are guaranteed by the Constitution and the Bill of Rights?
85. What is the introduction to the Constitution called?
86. Name one benefit of being a citizen of the United States.
87. What is the most important right granted to US citizens?
88. What is the United States Capitol?
89. What is the White House?
90. Where is the White House located?
91. What is the name of the President's official home?
92. Name one right guaranteed by the first amendment.
93. Who is the Commander in Chief of the US Military?
94. Which President was the first Commander in Chief of the US Military?
95. In what month do we vote for the President?
96. In what month is the new President inaugurated?
97. How many times may a senator be re-elected?

98. How many times may a congressman be re-elected?
99. What are the two major political parties in the US today?
100. How many States are there in the United States?

ANSWERS

1. Red, white and blue
2. 50
3. White
4. One for each State in the Union
5. 13
6. Red and white
7. They represent the original 13 States
8. 50
9. Independence Day
10. 4th July
11. England
12. England
13. George Washington
14. Name of current president
15. Name of current vice-president
16. The electoral college
17. Vice President
18. Four years
19. The Supreme Law of the Land
20. Yes
21. Amendments
22. 26
23. 3
24. Legislative, Executive and Judiciary
25. Congress
26. Congress
27. The Senate and the House of Representatives
28. To make laws
29. The people
30. 100
31. (Insert local information)
32. 6 years
33. 435
34. 2 years
35. The President, Cabinet, and departments under the cabinet members

36. The Supreme Court
37. To interpret laws
38. The Constitution
39. The first 10 amendments of the Constitution
40. (Insert local information)
41. (Insert local information)
42. Speaker of the House of Representatives
43. John Roberts
44. Connecticut, New Hampshire, New York, New Jersey, Massachusetts, Pennsylvania, Delaware, Virginia, North Carolina, South Carolina, Georgia, Rhode Island and Maryland
45. Patrick Henry
46. Germany, Italy and Japan
47. Hawaii and Alaska
48. 2
49. A civil rights leader
50. (Insert local information)
51. Must be a natural born citizen of the United States; must be at least 35 years old by the time he/she will serve; must have lived in the United States for at least 14 years
52. 2 from each State
53. Appointed by the President
54. 9
55. For religious freedom
56. Governor
57. Mayor
58. Thanksgiving
59. Thomas Jefferson
60. 4th July 1776
61. That all men are created equal
62. The *Star-Spangled Banner*
63. Francis Scott Key
64. The Bill of Rights
65. 18
66. The President
67. The Supreme Court
68. Abraham Lincoln
69. Freed the slaves
70. The Cabinet
71. George Washington
72. Form N-400, 'Application to file petition for naturalization'

73. The American Indians (Native Americans)
74. *The Mayflower*
75. Colonies
76. A. The right of freedom of speech, press, religion, peaceable assembly and requesting change of government.
    B. The right to bear arms (the right to have weapons or own a gun, though subject to certain regulations).
    C. The government may not quarter, or house, soldiers in people's homes during peacetime without the people's consent.
    D. The government may not search or take a person's property without a warrant.
    E. A person may not be tried twice for the same crime and does not have to testify against him/herself.
    F. A person charged with a crime still has some rights, such as the right to a trial and to have a lawyer.
    G. The right to trial by jury in most cases.
    H. Protects people against excessive or unreasonable fines or cruel and unusual punishment.
    I. The people have rights other than those mentioned in the Constitution.
    J. Any power not given to the federal government by the Constitution is a power of either the State or the people.
77. The Congress
78. Republic
79. Abraham Lincoln
80. 1787
81. The Bill of Rights
82. For countries to discuss and try to resolve world problems, to provide economic aid to many countries.
83. In the Capitol in Washington, D.C.
84. Everyone's (citizens and non-citizens living in the US)
85. The Preamble
86. Obtain federal government jobs, travel with a US passport, petition for close relatives to come to the US to live
87. The right to vote
88. The place where Congress meets
89. The President's official home
90. Washington D.C. (1600 Pennsylvania Avenue N.W.)

91. The White House
92. Freedom of speech, press, religion, peaceable assembly and requesting change of the government
93. The President
94. George Washington
95. November
96. January
97. There is no limit
98. There is no limit
99. Democratic and Republican
100. 50

Petition forms change so regularly that we decided against including them in this edition of the book. All forms are available on the US Bureau of Citizenship and Immigration Services (BCIS) website. Go to www.uscis.gov to download the latest forms.

Glossary

Please refer to the glossary for answers to any questions about the specialised terms used in this book.

Adjustment of Status. The procedures for changing to permanent residence status through the INS.

Advance Parole. Permission to leave the US and re-enter during adjustment of status procedures.

Alien Registration Card. Formal name for green card.

Application for Immigrant Visa and Alien Registration. The procedures for applying for immigrant status through a consulate.

Arrival Departure Card. Issued at port of entry to evidence legal status.

Bilateral Investment Treaty, Friendship Commerce and **Navigation Treaties.** The agreements between the US and a foreign government which enable treaty trader or treaty investor status.

Change of Status. An application to the USCIS to change from one nonimmigrant status to another nonimmigrant status.

Consulates. Representative offices of a foreign country located in major cities of the host country. Consulates take care of trade, economic, political and visa issues.

Consuls. Foreign service employees who work in embassies and consulates. Consuls issue visas.

Department of State. The agency of the United States government responsible for managing its foreign affairs. This agency controls the issuing of visas for travel to the US.

Embassy. The representative office of a foreign country located in the capital city of the host country. Embassies take care of political, trade, economic and visa issues. An

155

ambassator is the head of post at an embassy.

Essential Skill. A skill, essential to the success of the enterprise, that is generally unavailable in the US.

Executive. The person who establishes corporate goals and policies, and monitors the managers.

Extension of Stay. An application to the USCIS to extend the stay period listed on Form I-94.

Green Card. Common name for alien registration card for permanent residence.

I-94 Card. The form issued to temporary visitors to the US as evidence of their immigration status and allowed period of stay within the US.

Immigrant. A person who wants to live in the US for an indefinite period of time or permanently.

Immigration and Naturalization Service (USCIS). A sub-agency of the US Department of Justice responsible for controlling immigration within the US.

International organisation. A foreign and US company(ies) linked by 50 per cent or more common ownership.

Labor Certification. The process for determining that no US workers meet the offered job's minimum requirements. Unless exempted, labor certification is a prerequisite for employment-based green card categories.

Labor Conditions Application Process. A form filed with the Department of Labor for the purpose of notifying US workers that a foreign worker will be employed at the job site. Also used for the purpose of ensuring that the US employer is not hiring a foreign worker at less than the wages normally paid to US workers for the same position.

Manager. A person who manages other managers, supervisors or professionals within a business organisation. Managers implement corporate goals and policies through subordinates.

Multiple Entry Visa. Allows more than one entry into US.

Naturalization. The process for becoming a US citizen.

Nonimmigrant Status. A temporary status limited to a particular purpose for a set period of time.

Petition. Generic name for the forms used by the USCIS to determine eligibility for various visa categories.

Preference system. System for allocating permanent residence visas by skills or family relationship.

Prevailing wage. The wage, determined by the Department of Labor, normally paid to US workers for a particular job.

Practical Training. A programme available to students that permits them to work in the US after or during university study.

Quota System. The system used to limit the number of visas available to each country for particular visa classifications.

Pilot Visa Waiver Program. An agreement with several countries and the US that permits each other's nationals to enter the country for business or pleasure purposes without a visa for up to 90 days.

Professionals. Persons with at least a four-year university degree, or equivalent in experience and education, in a recognised professional discipline such as accounting, law, engineering or the sciences.

Re-entry Permit. A declaration of one's intention to maintain US permanent residence during prolonged absences from the US.

Specialised knowledge. A narrowly-held skill which helps the US employer's ability to compete in international markets.

Treaty Investment. Substantial investment in the US made by treaty companies or individuals.

Treaty Trade. Substantial trade between the US and a foreign country.

US Citizenship and Immigration Services (USCIS). A law enforcement agency; part of the Homeland Security Department.

Visa. Permission to apply for entry to a country, usually issued by a country's foreign service.

Visa Revalidation. An application to the Visa Office in Washington, D.C. for a new visa of the same type.

Visa Waiver. Entry to US without a visa – certain countries qualify.

Index

Adjustment of Status to
    Permanent Residence, 73
Advance Parole, 73, 94
Alien Registration Card, 7, 69,
    73
Application for Immigrant Visa
    and Alien Registration, 16,
    32
Application Procedure –
    (Documentation, 144)
  B1 Visa, 16
  B2 Visa, 20
  K1 Visa, 24
  E, H and L Visa, 26, 35, 41,
    88
  N400 – Citizenship Test, 128
  Self Assessment, 125
Arrival/Departure Card, 9

Baby Droppers, 126
Bilateral Investment Treaty
    (BIT), 31
Businesses (setting up in the
    US), 42, 52

Children, 50
Citizenship, 126
Citizenship Test, 128, 148
Certificate of Naturalisation,
    129
Corporate Executives, 86

Denied Entry, 10
Death Taxes, 42
Department of Labor (DOL),
    71, 94, 98, 99
Department of State, 7

Dependent Employers, 36
Direct Trade, 33
Discrimination, 66
Dole, 71
Dual Citizenship, 127

Employee Criteria, 80, 96–104,
    134
Employee Relocation, 134
Employment Authorisation
    Card, 73, 116
Employment Creation Aliens
    Programme, 79
Engineers, 58
Exemption (National Interest),
    96
Expiration Dates, 9
Extended Stay, 11, 48

Family Class, 75
Fiancé(e) Applications, 24
Friendship Commerce and
    Navigation Treaty (FCN),
    31

Green Card, 6, 68, (categories,
    74), 78, 90, 93, 109, 110

Illegal Aliens, 13, 76
Illness, 72, 133
Immigrant Investor
    Programme, 3, 78–85
Immigration and Nationality
    Act, 17
Immigration Forms, 139
Internal Revenue Service
    (IRS), 107
Investing in America, 78

Job Requirements, 98

Labor Certification, 85, 95, 98, 99, 104
Labor Conditions Application (LCA), 36

Managers, 53, 85
Media Industry Visas, 118
Melting Pot, 129
Mini Green Card, 119
Ministers, 121

National Visa Center, 93, 142
Naturalisation, 126
North American Free Trade Agreement (NAFTA), 12, 123

One Year Rule, 48–9
Overstays, 10, 11

Permanent Residence Visa (See Green Card)
Practical Training Programme, 116–17
Preference System, 2
Priority Date, 70, 105
Professional Licences, 37

Quota System, 1, 70, 75

Recruiting, 104
Regional Centres, 82
Religious Workers, 122
Relocation Tips, 134
Retirement, 85
Revalidation of Visa, 12

Schooling, 112
Self Assessment, 125
State Benefit Recipients, 71
Students, 20
Studying and Working, 115

Tax Returns, 107

Technicians, 62
Temporary Working Visa (explained), 26
Treaty Company, 31
Treaty National Status, 123
Two Step Programme, 85

USCIS, 4, 69, 92–7
USCIS Centres, 142

Visa (full category listing, 139)
  B-1 – Business Trips, 16, 125
  B-2 – Visiting for Pleasure, 20, 76, 125
  Free Trade Act, 12
  E-1 – Treaty Trader, 32, 46, 50–4, 76, 117, 124
  E-2 – Treaty Investor, 33, 46, 52–4, 76, 117, 124
  F-1 – Students, 78, 112
  H-1B – Professional Worker, 34–41, 53–8, 76, 117, 124
  H-2B – Technical Worker, 62–3
  H, **L**, and **E** – explained, 40–1
  I – Information Media, 7, 118
  Immigrant (Non-Immigrant), 6, 13, 87, 92
  Investor, 78, 84
  K-1 – Fiancé(e) Category, 24
  L – Intra-Company Transfer, 28, 60–1, 124–5
  L-1A – Manager, 52–3, 88–90
  L-1B – Specialised Knowledge, 60
  M-1 – Vocational Programme, 112–14
  Multiple Entry, 9
  O – Outstanding People, 119, 125
  Permanent Residence, 6, 69, 72, 73, 106
Petitions, 8, 75

P – Professionals (Athletes, Musicians, Entertainers), 120
Q – Cultural Exchange, 120
Re-Entry Permits, 106
R – Religious Workers, 121
V – Spouse, three year wait, 77
Revalidation, 12
Social Security Number (SSN), 110

Status (change of), 11
Student Criteria, 113, 117
Tax Identification Number (TIN), 111
Travelling (Ref. student), 113
Treaty Trader, 12, 29–34
Treaty Investor, 12, 29–34
Visitor for Pleasure, 20, 125
Waiver, 6, 77, 96

Young Adults, 21